GLOBETROTTER

TRAVEL GUIDE

DUBLIN

ROBIN GAULDIE

NEW
HOLLAND

GLOBETROTTER
TRAVEL GUIDE

First edition published in 1997
by New Holland (Publishers) Ltd.
London • Cape Town • Sydney • Singapore

Reprinted 1997

24 Nutford Place
London W1H 6DQ
United Kingdom

80 McKenzie Street
Cape Town 8001
South Africa

3/2 Aquatic Drive
Frenchs Forest, NSW 2086
Australia

ISBN 1 85368 804 5

Commissioning Editor: Tim Jollands
Managing Editor: Clive During
Editors: Laurence Lemmon-Warde,
Anna Bennett
Design and DTP: Laurence Lemmon-Warde
Cartographer: Eloise Moss
Compiler/Verifier: Elaine Fick
Picture Researcher: Emily Hedges

Reproduction by cmyk prepress
Printed and bound in Hong Kong by Sing Cheong
Printing Co. Ltd.

Photographic Credits: Bord Failte Photo/Brian Lynch,
pages 86, 87, 89, 100, 105, 112; Bord Failte Photo/Pat
Odea, page 88; Dept. of Arts, Culture and the
Gaeltacht, page 101; Norma Joseph, pages 32 (top left
& right), 38 (top), 108 (top and bottom), 109; The Kobal
Collection, page 30 (top); Life File/Fraser Ralston,
page 42; Life File/J Searle, pages 39; The Mansell
Collection, pages 8, 10, 11, 12, 13, 16, 17; Robert
Harding Picture Library (RHPL), cover (bottom
right), pages 9, 22, 57, 60; RHPL/C Bowman, page 55;
RHPL/ Phillip Craven, pages 40 (bottom), 41 (top), 48,
78, 95; RHPL/ Michael Jenner, pages 44, 74, 76, 77,
107 (bottom), 81 (left & right); RHPL/J Lightfoot, title
page, pages 28, 34, 37, 50 (bottom), 98; RHPL/Duncan
Maxwell, cover (top right and bottom left), pages 6,
21, 26 (top and bottom), 56, 58, 61, 66 (top), 70, 72, 73
(bottom), 75; RHPL/ HP Merten, page 14; RHPL/L
Proud, page 54; RHPL/ Roy Rainford, page 27;
RHPL/Rolf Richardson, pages 20, 31, 62;
RHPL/Michael Short, pages 102, 107 (top), 83;
RHPL/Liam White, page 90; RHPL/Adam Woolfitt,
pages 7 (bottom left), 41 (bottom), 110, 111; RHPL/Earl
Young, page 66 (bottom); Peter Ryan, cover (top left),
pages 7 (bottom right), 15, 18, 23, 24, 33, 40 (top), 43, 47,
49, 50 (top), 51, 52, 53, 63, 64, 65, 67, 68, 69, 73 (top),
106; The Slide File, pages 25, 82, 84, 85, 93, 97, 113;
Peter Wilson, pages 4, 29, 30 (bottom), 38 (bottom), 114.

Cover photographs:
Top left: *Pool Beg Lighthouse on Dublin Bay.*
Top right: *An aerial view of Dublin city.*
Bottom left: *Beautiful Phoenix Park, the largest
city park in Europe.*
Bottom right: *Enjoying a pint in the Stag's Head
pub, one of Dublin's more than 700 inner-city
drinking establishments.*
Title page: *The O'Connell Bridge straddles the
River Liffey in central Dublin.*

CONTENTS

1
Introducing
Dublin

Dublin (or *Baile Ath Cliath*, as it is known in Irish Gaelic) capital of the Republic of Ireland, has a reputation out of all proportion to its small size. With a population of just over one million and an area of only 50km² (20 sq miles), the lively city on the **River Liffey** has given birth to far more than its fair share of authors, poets, playwrights, satirists, musicians and politicians. Dubliners are renowned for their ready wit and full-time commitment to having a good time; they offer visitors a warm welcome and, small though it is, Dublin has plenty of historic and contemporary sights to see and a variety of exciting things to do. One of the city's delights is that many of its greatest attractions are packed close together in the city centre, few of them more than ten minutes' walk from each other.

While Dublin is an historic city, it is also a very modern one. The grand public buildings, wide streets and elegant squares date from its Georgian heyday, but Dublin in the 1990s is cosmopolitan in the best sense of the word. Membership of the **European Union** has changed Ireland for the better in many ways, and the Irish capital's own unique culture borrows the best from all over Europe and adds an inimitable touch of Irishness. Dublin's nightlife is legendary, as anyone who has run the gauntlet of the lively nightspots of **Leeson Street** will tell you. But the city's biggest attraction is simply the 'crack' – not an illicit substance but an addictive blend of loquacious wit, ready satire, high-flown verbal imagery and saloon-bar philosophy to which native Dubliners remain firmly committed.

TOP ATTRACTIONS

*** Christ Church Cathedral: Ancient cathedral with historic statues and tombs.
*** St Patrick's Cathedral.
*** Trinity College: A pageant of Irish history housed in a gracious 400-year-old building.
*** Guinness Brewery: The home of Ireland's most famous product.
** Kilmainham Gaol: Eerie memorial to those who died in Ireland's long independence struggle.
** Dublin Castle: Viking and British relics.
** Phoenix Park: Historic buildings, riverside walks and a fine zoo.

Opposite: *Bustling High Street.*

Above: *Dublin city centre, on the River Liffey.*
Opposite left: *Enjoying conversation in a cosy Dublin bar.*
Opposite right: *A lighthouse on Dublin Bay.*

FACT FILE

Dublin is on the Republic of Ireland's east coast, facing the Irish Sea and straddling the mouth of the River Liffey. The city is both flat and compact, making it ideal for sightseeing on foot. The historic city centre lies south of the Liffey. Dublin's more prosperous residential areas lie south of the centre, while poorer, working-class areas tend to cluster on the northern outskirts. The population of Dublin City and County is 1,025,304 (1991 Census).

THE LAND

Where Dublin city now stands on Ireland's east coast, three rivers – the **Liffey**, the **Tolka** and the **Dodder** – once flowed into the Irish Sea, creating a wide marshy delta around Dublin Bay. Land reclamation and natural silting have partially filled this delta, so that central Dublin is now several kilometres from the open waters of Dublin Bay, which is sheltered by the granite headlands of Howth in the north and Killiney in the south.

Dublin city is divided in two by the River Liffey, with its historic heart on the river's south bank. Two canals, the **Royal Canal** and the **Grand Canal**, built in the 18th century, form a ring round the centre.

Surrounding the capital is **County Dublin**, an eastern extension of the central Irish plain, with a scattering of castles, pretty villages, and country towns within 20 minutes of the city centre. Equally nearby are the charming harbour towns and seaside resorts of Dublin Bay and the Irish Sea coast. South of the capital are the low ranges of the **Dublin Mountains**, while to the north is rich farming country and a coastline of long sandy beaches interspersed with pretty river estuaries.

Dublin really is a city which offers the visitor the best of all possible worlds, from the bustle of a sophisticated, small European metropolis to unspoiled countryside and windswept beaches.

Climate

Ireland has mild, wet winters and temperate wet summers thanks to the influence of the surrounding Atlantic Ocean and the Gulf Stream. Dublin, like the rest of the country, can be visited all year round.

DUBLIN	J	F	M	A	M	J	J	A	S	O	N	D
MAX TEMP. °C	0	1	7	12	18	21	22	22	18	12	5	1
MIN TEMP. °C	-5	-4	-1	3	8	11	13	13	9	5	1	-3
MAX TEMP. °F	32	34	45	54	64	70	72	72	64	54	41	34
MIN TEMP. °F	23	25	30	37	46	52	55	55	48	41	34	27
HOURS OF SUN DAILY	2	2.5	5	6	8	8.5	9	8	6	4	2	1
RAINFALL mm	18	18	18	27	48	54	68	55	31	33	20	21
RAINFALL in	0.7	0.7	0.7	1.1	1.9	2.1	2.7	2.2	1.2	1.3	0.8	0.8
DAYS OF RAINFALL	13	11	10	11	13	12	13	12	10	13	12	13

Sub-zero temperatures in the city centre are rare, as is snow. It is also very unusual for summer temperatures to climb above 20°C (68°F) and rain is a possibility at any time of year. The Irish capital is not a city to visit with sunbathing in mind and the waters of the nearby Irish Sea, inviting though they may look, are cold enough to deter all but the hardiest, even in midsummer. That said, Dublin in winter – unlike many other European capitals – imposes no great hardships on the visitor and when the weather turns really nasty there is always a cosy nearby bar or café to duck into.

In general, Ireland's weather is even more erratic than that of the neighbouring British Isles. In common with the rest of Europe, there are four very distinct seasons: spring (April–May), summer (June–September) autumn (October–November) and winter (December–March). July and August are the hottest months of the year, January and February the coldest.

Top Ten Things To Do

- Get a taste for **Guinness** at the Hop Store.
- Try **Irish whiskey** at Jameson's Distillery.
- Follow in **James Joyce's** footsteps on a guided walk.
- Go to a traditional **Irish music pub**.
- Trace your Irish ancestry.
- Spend a day at the **races**.
- Wander through lively **street markets**.
- Take a walk in the **Dublin Mountains.**
- Go skinny-dipping at the **Forty Foot beach**.
- Dine on fabulous **fresh seafood**.

Above: *St Patrick arrives in Ireland.*
Opposite: *Beautiful Viking jewellery.*

HISTORY IN BRIEF

Founded by **Viking invaders** in the 10th century, Dublin was a wealthy, cosmopolitan trading port at a time when much of the rest of Ireland was forest and bogland. From Norse hands Dublin passed to the Anglo-Norman king, Henry II, and for at least 400 years thereafter the city was a frequently-besieged English stronghold in a hostile land. Even after the whole of Ireland was more or less pacified, Dublin, as the seat of an alien government, was very different in character from other Irish towns.

From Prehistory to Christianity

Ireland's fascinating prehistory has been both preserved and revealed by the widespread use of turf (peat), a semi-fossil fuel dug from the boglands of the country's central plain. Prehistoric human remains, tools and weapons found during turf-digging indicate Ireland was first settled as the last ice age withdrew from northern Europe, around 9000BC.

The first **Celtic** people began to arrive in Ireland during the first millennium BC, and had much in common with the Celts of the British Isles and Gaul (now France). Unlike their neighbours in what is now England, however, they escaped conquest by the Roman Empire and – when it collapsed – by Anglo-Saxon invaders from northern Europe. Instead, Ireland preserved a uniquely Celtic way of life with no towns and very few permanent buildings.

In the late fourth or early fifth century, **Christianity** came to Ireland, probably through Irish trade with the Christian British settlements in Wales. Traditionally, however, its bringer was **St Patrick** (369–461). Christianity expanded steadily in Ireland during the

---

ANCIENT MYTHS

Irish legends of the *Tuatha de Danaan*, the *Fir Bolg* and other half-magical races and heroes may reflect the complex world of Ireland in the first millennium BC. The first Celtic incomers began to arrive during this era, but are believed to have been only one of several ethnic groups then inhabiting the island. Their bronze and iron weapons and tools may have made them seem magically powerful to the stone-using people who were there when they arrived, and the legends contain many references to magically sharp swords and spears.

sixth, seventh and eighth centuries, and the powerful monastic orders which grew up during this period came to rival the Irish kings.

The Vikings

Dublin enters the annals of Ireland late, with the coming of the Vikings to this coast. The first Viking longships appeared in AD795, and for the next 40 years Viking raiders struck again and again, raiding monasteries for their treasures and farmlands for their cattle. Most of the invaders came from Norway, and in later centuries from the Viking colonies in Orkney, Iceland and the Hebrides. **Dublin Bay**, with the mouth of the Liffey forming a natural harbour on the Irish Sea, was an ideal base for their raiding fleets. In 841–842 Vikings began to establish a permanent, year-round settlement on the south bank of the Liffey, and Norse graves found in **Kilmainham cemetery** date from this era. Though driven out in 902, the Norse returned to recapture the settlement in 925 and for the next two centuries the Norse kings of Dublin and rival Viking settlements in Limerick and Waterford were a permanent fixture on the Irish scene, fighting among themselves and frequently in alliance with native Irish rulers.

Brian Boru

The Viking invaders had been aided by the ongoing small wars between Ireland's dozens of princelings. Brian Boru, the great Irish warrior king, was the first leader to

VIKING DUBLIN

The Dublin Norse were keener traders than raiders and commerce with the Baltic, North Sea and Mediterranean ports made Dublin one of western Europe's wealthiest seaports for almost 300 years. Excavations on the site of Viking Dublin have turned up 10th-century gold and silver coins and glassware from Scandinavia. Later 12th-century finds indicate that by then Dublin was trading with England and Normandy. Dublin in the 11th and 12th centuries was a substantial town, defended by stone ramparts and ruled by Christianized Norse kings who had intermarried with noble Irish families.

HIGH KINGS

Well into the Christian era, scores of petty kingdoms – most of them no larger than one of Ireland's smaller counties today – vied with each other for power and prestige and paid lip service to the rule of a high king or *ri ruirech*, who might control as much as a quarter of the island which then, as now, was divided into four large provinces – Ulster, Leinster, Munster and Connaught. The ceremonial seat of the High King was at the Hill of Tara, not far from modern Dublin, and is still marked by a ring of ancient standing stones.

come close to bringing the entire island under his sway. By the second half of the 10th century Boru was styling himself King of North Munster and after 25 years of almost continual warfare was able to proclaim himself High King of Tara, traditional seat of the most powerful of all the kings of Ireland. In 997 he took Dublin, defeating a revolt by the Dublin Vikings in 999.

In 1013 his greatest rival, **Mael Morda**, King of Leinster, rose against him, bringing in a huge army of mercenary Vikings. They met in battle at **Clontarf** – now a north Dublin suburb – on Good Friday 1014. Irish and Viking chroniclers record that the battle was fierce even by the standards of those bloody times. Though Boru's army won the day, slaying both Mael Morda and the Viking Earl Sigurd of Norway, both Boru and his son and heir, Murchadh, also fell. The battle is often claimed as an Irish victory which ended the threat of Viking conquest, though in fact the Viking star was no longer ascendant, and Vikings fought (as usual) on both sides. Long after Clontarf, Dublin remained in the hands of Viking rulers, one of whom, **Sitric Silkenbeard**, gave the city its first cathedral, founding Christ Church in 1038.

There was no contender strong enough to take up Boru's campaign to bring Ireland under one king, and the island disintegrated once again into a patchwork of squabbling minor rulers. One of them was Brian Boru's great grandson **Muirchertach** (1086–1119) who seized the former Viking kingdom of Dublin.

THE WOOD QUAY

In the late 1970s the Dublin Corporation, which manages the city, decided to build a vast new office complex beside the River Liffey. Early work uncovered Ireland's oldest **Viking site** – remnants of the walls and streets of the oldest settlement where Dublin now stands. Despite protests, court battles and a brief occupation of the site, building went ahead and much of Dublin's Viking heritage was lost forever.

The Normans

A generation after Clontarf, William the Bastard, Duke of Normandy, made himself King of England at the head of a band of land-hungry conquerors who over the next century, fanned out into England, Wales and Scotland. By the mid 12th century, some of them were casting hungry eyes on Ireland.

Their opportunity came when **Dermot McMurrough** (1134–71), King of Leinster, sought Norman help in his war with **Rory O'Connor**, King of Connaught. Henry II of England (1154–89) allowed McMurrough to recruit Norman lords from Wales, led by the Earl of Pembroke, **Richard FitzGilbert de Clare** (1130–76). Nicknamed 'Strongbow', the earl recruited a Norman invasion force and in 1170 landed at Baginbun in County Wexford, capturing Dublin in September of the same year. In 1171 King Henry himself landed in Ireland – his aim apparently to curb any ambitions Strongbow might have to make himself king of Ireland – and in 1172 took Dublin under royal protection. In 1177 Henry proclaimed his son John (later King John II of England), Lord of Ireland.

The Norman barons gradually brought more of the country under their control, but vast areas of Ireland were covered with bog and thick forest in which their warhorses and chainmail were virtually useless. Beyond the Pale – an earth wall thrown up to protect Dublin and the surrounding counties – their control of the countryside was often tenuous, and in much of Ireland the Irish kings still ruled unchallenged. Meanwhile, the Anglo-Norman conquerors were influenced by their Irish subjects, adopted Irish

Opposite: *An attack on Ireland by the Danes.*
Below: *A view of Dublin Bay including Clontarf, where the famous battle was fought in 1014. Many of the great Viking chiefs perished at Clontarf and tales of the fighting spread throughout the Norse world.*

DUBLIN'S NAMES

Dublin's Irish toponym, *Baile Ath Cliath* – 'the town of the hurdle ford' – dates from early Celtic times, when **Conor MacNessa**, King of Ulster, built a ford of woven tree-branches to cross the River Liffey on his way to battle with the rival King of Leinster. The modern name comes from '*Dubh Linn*', meaning 'black pool', the Irish name for the stretch of the Liffey where the Vikings built their first permanent settlement.

as their native tongue, married into Irish noble families, and gradually became more Irish than English. In Dublin, the first Dublin Castle was built between 1208 and 1220 on a low hill commanding the Liffey and the settlement on either bank.

In 1316 Ireland was drawn into the war between England and Scotland when Edward Bruce, brother of the Scottish King Robert, invaded Ireland and had himself crowned king. His Scots army came close to taking Dublin before it was defeated, and Bruce killed, at Faughart in 1318.

The **Wars of the Roses**, between the English noble houses of Lancaster and York, left the Anglo-Irish earls free to rule as they chose in Dublin and the Pale without interference from the English crown, and the Fitzgerald family of Kildare emerged as the most potent force in Anglo-Irish affairs.

From the 16th to the 18th century

By the first quarter of the 16th century, the Anglo-Irish were virtually independent of the English crown. With England's conversion to the protestant faith under Henry VIII, the struggle for Ireland took a new turn. The Anglo-Irish settlers and the native Irish remained staunchly Catholic, and for the first time religious as well as politi-

Below: *An early map of the city of Dublin.*

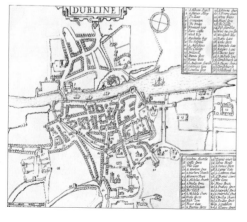

cal and military conflict became an issue. In 1541 **Henry VIII** declared himself King of Ireland – previous English monarchs had used the title Lord of Ireland – and decreed that all Irish lands were crown property. When Catholic Spain set out to crush heretic England in the reign of Elizabeth I, it found ready allies in Ireland. The country was ravaged by war as the Irish and Anglo-Irish rebelled against the crown again and again.

The most dangerous rising of the era was led by **Hugh O'Neill**, Earl of Tyrone (1540–1616). Though he was at first a protégé of the English, accepting his earldom from Elizabeth I in 1585, he turned against the crown in 1598, in alliance with the O'Donnell clan.

Above: *An engraving of Dublin Bay.*

Under Elizabeth I, England began the first systematic campaigns to conquer Ireland thoroughly and completely by destroying the traditional Irish way of life, which the English had come to see as barbaric. Already, Dublin had become in many ways an English city, with the strongest garrison in Ireland and a large English merchant community.

In 1642 the English Civil War broke out and Ireland was drawn into the complicated and bloody struggle between the forces of the Crown and Parliament.

The Cromwellian regime was followed by the return of the Stewart dynasty to the throne in the person of Charles II, but strong anti-Catholic feeling in England brought little hope for the Irish. On the positive side, Charles II's Lord Lieutenant of Ireland, the Duke of Ormond, began to plan and develop Dublin, building a second bridge across the Liffey and stone quays along the south bank of the river.

Catholic hopes were raised when James II, brother of Charles II, came to the throne in 1685. James was a Catholic and intended to restore the Roman Church in both England and Ireland. In 1688, however, the English parliament toppled James and invited the Dutch prince, **William of Orange**, who was married to James's daughter Mary, to take the throne. James fled to Ireland to seek Catholic support, plunging the country once more into turmoil. In 1690, however, his army was defeated at the River Boyne, and William completed his triumph with a second victorious campaign in 1691.

CROMWELL'S MASSACRES

In 1649 Oliver Cromwell, Lord Protector of England, arrived in Ireland with 20,000 battle-hardened soldiers. Cromwell's troops crushed the rebellion with extreme savagery. At the siege of Drogheda, north of Dublin, they massacred more than 1000 men, women and children, and at Wexford some 2000 inhabitants were slaughtered. Other strongholds in rebel hands quickly surrendered for fear of further massacres.

With this latest Catholic defeat, the Protestant minority in Ireland gained an ascendancy that would last throughout the 18th century and well into the 19th.

Dublin, as the seat of government, became the centre of Irish Protestant culture and politics. The Dublin parliament, with a permanent Protestant majority, banished Catholic clergy and debarred Catholics from teaching, marrying Protestants, or taking court action in land cases. Throughout Ireland, Catholics were dispossessed of their land. The capital had grown by 1700 into a fair-sized city, home to 50,000 people, with a cultural and economic life as energetic as any city in Europe. Dublin in the 18th century underwent a remarkable transformation from a medieval garrison town, always prepared for siege or rebellion, into one of the most elegant cities in Europe. The Protestant merchant class, political elite, and rural aristocracy competed to build the most imposing town houses, villas and public buildings. Among the leading architects of Georgian Dublin was James Gandon, who designed the three most striking buildings in Dublin – the Four Courts, the Custom House, and the King's Inns – between 1781 and 1808. He also designed the east portico of the Parliament building, now the Bank of Ireland.

DANIEL O'CONNELL

Daniel O'Connell (1775–1847) was the first and greatest of non-violent campaigners for Irish home rule. O'Connell campaigned for an independent Irish parliament which would reflect the Catholic majority but remain subject to the British Crown, as well as for rural land reform. His mass rallies made him a formidable figure, and his election to Parliament in 1828 forced the British government to allow **Catholics** to become members of parliament. O'Connell's campaigning for the repeal of the Act of Union led to his being arrested and charged with conspiracy in 1846. Briefly imprisoned, he went into exile in Italy, where he died the following year.

The Protestant Irish elite known as the **Ascendancy** were dominant throughout the 18th century, maintaining a gracious way of life at the expense of their Irish tenantry. As the century wore on, their demands for the right to pass separate laws for Ireland grew louder. In 1782, this was granted, marking the high point of the Ascendancy's power.

The infectious libertarian ideas of the French revolution encouraged a a group led by the Dublin-born Protestant **Wolfe Tone** (1763–98) to form the **United Irishmen**, whose aim was to bring Protestant and Catholic communities together to campaign for parliamentary reform. Banned in 1796, the United Irishmen became a revolutionary movement aligned with Republican France, where Tone fled to seek support for an independent Irish republic.

Tone's rebellion, in 1798, was a pathetic affair, backed by only 1000 French troops. Faced by vastly stronger British forces, defeat inevitably followed.

The Act of Union
In 1800 the British government dismantled the Irish parliament and initiated direct rule from London, uniting the two kingdoms of England and Ireland by the Act of Union which took effect from 1801.

BRAZEN HEAD

Walking along Bridge Street, in the heart of old Dublin, look out for The Brazen Head, Dublin's oldest pub. A venerable whitewashed building, it has stood here since 1688, though it is claimed that there has been an inn on the spot since the very earliest times. In the 1790s it was patronized by conspirators of **Wolfe Tone's** revolutionary movement, the **United Irishmen** – as well as by government agents who eavesdropped on their conversations, arrested them and destroyed the movement.

Opposite: *The Custom House, restored and reopened in 1991.*
Below: *Typical Georgian doorways.*

OLIVER PLUNKETT

Oliver Plunkett, Archbishop of Dublin, was martyred in 1678, a victim of the so-called Popish Plot invented by the English agitator Titus Oates, who whipped up mob hysteria claiming Spain and the papacy were conspiring to conquer England. Plunkett was arrested and executed after a show trial in which he was found guilty on trumped up charges of plotting to overthrow English rule with Spanish help. He was eventually canonized by the Catholic Church.

Charles Stewart Parnell (1846–91) was educated at Cambridge, joined the Irish Parliamentary Party in 1874 and was elected MP for Meath a year later. Over the next three years he built an alliance of all the groups supporting home rule for Ireland and in 1879 formed the National Land League to campaign for land to be handed over to peasant farmers. By the mid 1880s Parnell was at the height of his powers, bargaining with British prime minister William Ewart Gladstone for home rule in return for support for Gladstone's Liberal government, but in 1890 he was ruined by the exposure of his long affair with a married woman, Kitty O'Shea. He spoke in public for the last time in 1891 and died soon after.

Throughout the 19th century, peaceful agitation and campaigning for the return of Irish affairs to the control of an elected Dublin parliament was paralleled by less-disciplined revolts, mainly in rural areas. The first of these was in 1803. Led by a republican idealist and former United Irishman named Robert Emmett (1778– 1803), a tiny force of 90 men (Emmett had hoped for 2000) set out to attack Dublin Castle. They never had a chance, and were quickly rounded up and transported or hanged.

The greatest of those advocating peaceful means was Daniel O'Connell (1775–1847) who campaigned for an independent Irish parliament which would reflect the Catholic majority in Ireland but remain subject to the British Crown. O'Connell's mass rallies made him a formidable political figure, and his election to Parliament in 1828 forced the British government to allow Catholics to become Members of Parliament.

O'Connell continued to campaign for the repeal of the Act of Union, but in 1846 he was arrested and charged with conspiracy. Briefly imprisoned, he went into exile in Italy, where he died in 1847.

The Famine

Perhaps the most significant and certainly the most highly symbolic event of the first half of the 19th century was the great potato famine which struck Ireland between 1845 and 1849. By the 1840s, Ireland's peasantry had completely abandoned traditional forms of cultivation and were wholly dependent on the potato, introduced from North America during the 17th and 18th centuries. In many parts of the country, ordinary people ate virtually nothing else. When the potato crop was struck by blight in 1845, the result was famine, made worse by the British government's reluctance or inability to provide alternative food supplies.

Hundreds of thousands of people starved. Millions emigrated during the famine and in the years that followed. In a sense, Ireland has never really recovered. In 1841 it was one of the most densely populated countries in Europe, with a population of around eight million. Today, its population is little more than half that.

The bitter anger which followed the famine stiffened the Irish nationalist movement. In 1858 the Fenian movement, launched by James Stephens, picked up the banner of armed resistance to English rule and Fenian risings punctuated the second half of the 19th century. The constitutional nationalists were led for most of this time by **Charles Stewart Parnell**, a Protestant and the Member of Parliament for West Meath, whose grass-roots campaigning for a fairer system of rents and land tenure for the Irish peasant won him widespread support and he pursued his demands for Home Rule for Ireland. In 1881 Parnell's demands for Irish freedom led to his imprisonment in Kilmainham Gaol in Dublin, from where he continued to write and campaign. He was released in 1882 on condition that he work against rural violence, but a shaky alliance between Parnell and the British government of William Ewart Gladstone's Liberal Party was wrecked when a group of extremists known as the Invincibles murdered Lord Frederick Cavendish, British chief secretary for Ireland, in Phoenix Park.

In 1905 **Arthur Griffith** launched Sinn Fein, a party calling for an independent Irish Parliament in Dublin. In northern Ireland, the most strongly Protestant part of the country, fiercely anti-nationalist Protestants formed the Ulster Volunteer Force and began arming themselves to

Above: *An engraving of the Potato Famine.*
Opposite: *Charles Stewart Parnell.*

JONATHAN SWIFT

Jonathan Swift (1667–1745) was born in Dublin and educated at Trinity College, becoming dean of St Patrick's in 1713. A prolific author, he is best known for his fantasy **Gulliver's Travels** (1726) – the only one of his many works for which he received any payment, and the only one published under his own name. He is less fondly remembered for his outrageous (though satirical) suggestion that in time of famine the Irish should eat their own children. He left one third of his fortune to found a charitable institution, St Patrick's Hospital in Bow Lane, now a psychiatric hospital, and is buried in St Patrick's Cathedral.

resist any moves to make them part of a Catholic-dominated independent Ireland. In the south, nationalists formed themselves into the less well armed Irish Volunteers. Ireland seemed poised to topple into civil war when, in 1914, the outbreak of World War I temporarily united hardline Protestant loyalists and moderate nationalists behind the British government.

The Easter Rising

On Easter Monday 1916 the Irish Republican Brotherhood, forerunner of the Irish Republican Army, launched an armed attack on British forces in Dublin. The British response was to use overwhelming force. After six days of fighting the rebels surrendered. They had lost 64 dead and had killed 130 British soldiers, but the worst casualties were among the people of Dublin, 300 of whom died in the fighting.

The execution of fifteen of the rebel leaders, including **Padraic Pearse** and **James Connolly**, proved to be a mistake. Dublin was placed under martial law, and sympathy for the rebels increased. Militant republicanism dominated the nationalist movement. In the elections of 1918 Sinn Fein won 73 Irish seats, the Irish Nationalists six, and the loyalist Ulster Unionist Party 16, all in the north, thus setting the scene for the division of Ireland. Sinn Fein, instead of taking up its seats in London, declared its own Dail Eireann (Irish Assembly), presided over by Eamon de Valera.

War and Civil War

Between 1919 and 1920 the **IRA** waged a war of ambush and assassination against the officers of the Royal Irish Constabulary. In 1922 Britain, the Ulster Unionists and the

HISTORICAL CALENDAR

ca 9000BC First Stone Age people settle in Ireland.
500BC or later First bronze-using Celts settle in Ireland.
ca AD432 St Patrick begins his Christian mission to Ireland.
795–835 First Viking raids.
841–2 Vikings occupy site of Dublin and begin settlement.
840–900 Infighting between Vikings and Irish kings.
950 Under Viking rule, Dublin becomes one of Europe's richest cities.
951 Brian Boru becomes King of North Munster. Era of Irish dynastic wars.
1014 Battle of Clontarf. With Boru's death, Ireland again fragmented.
1086–1119 Boru's grandson Muirchertach King of Dublin.
1169–70 First Norman invasion of Ireland led by Richard FitzGilbert de Clare nicknamed Strongbow (1130–76).
1170 Strongbow takes Dublin.
1171 Henry II of England claims Ireland.
1199 Dublin and County Dublin under Anglo-Norman control.
13th century Process of Anglo-Norman conquest continues.
1316 Edward Bruce, brother of Robert Bruce, King of Scotland,

claims Irish throne. Scots briefly besiege Dublin.
1318 Bruce defeated and killed at Battle of Faughart.
1348 One third of Dublin's population die of the plague.
15th century English power in Ireland weakened as result of civil war in England.
1494 Sir Edward Poyning decrees Parliament subject to English Crown Council.
1536 Revolt of Earl of Kildare put down and Kildare executed.
1580–3 Revolt against Crown in Munster and Leinster.
1595–1601 Revolt of O'Neill of Ulster with Spanish support.
1647 Dublin falls to English Parliamentary forces.
1649 Cromwell sacks Drogheda.
1688–1691 War in Ireland between Catholic supporters of deposed James II of England and Protestant William III.
18th century Legislation restricting Catholic rights.
1791 Society of United Irishmen founded.
1798 Irish revolt with limited French support, Wolfe Tone arrested and executed.
1800 Act of Union makes Ireland part of United Kingdom.
1803 Emmett's rebellion.

1829 Legislation to permit Catholics to sit in Parliament.
1845 Great potato famine.
1848 'Young Ireland' revolt defeated.
1858 Formation of Irish Republican Brotherhood.
1859 Foundation of Fenian Brotherhood in USA.
1867 Fenian uprising crushed.
1873 Foundation of Home Rule League.
1881 Charles Stewart Parnell imprisoned in Kilmainham Gaol.
1882 Rebel terrorists assassinate Lord Frederick Cavendish.
1908 Formation of Sinn Fein.
1912 Third Irish Home Rule Bill.
1913 Irish Citizens Army formed.
1914 Outbreak of World War I. British government withdraws Home Rule Bill.
1916 Easter Rising in Dublin.
1918 Sinn Fein election victory; Dail Eireann (Irish Parliament) formed.
1921 Anglo-Irish Treaty agrees limited self-rule.
1922 Irish Free State founded.
1937 New constitution for Eire replaces Irish Free State.
1948 Ireland becomes a republic.
1990 Mary Robinson becomes Ireland's first woman president.
1995 Unbanning of divorce.

Dail agreed a treaty granting most of Ireland independence but allowing the six northern, Protestant-dominated counties of Londonderry, Antrim, Down, Armagh, Tyrone and Fermanagh to remain part of Britain. The Irish Free State was born.

The Free State was immediately plunged into civil war between a hardline IRA faction which refused to recognise the treaty and the forces of the new government. In 1923 Eamon de Valera agreed a cease-fire and surrender. The frontiers of the present Republic of Ireland were established.

Opposite: *A bust commemorating Countess Markiewicz, who, among other things, became the first woman elected to the British parliament.*

Independent Ireland

The Irish Free State, the first of Britain's colonies to gain its freedom since the American Revolution, retained constitutional ties with Britain for a further 26 years. In 1949 the Fine Gael government of John Costello severed all remaining ties with Britain, finally declaring Ireland an independent republic outside the British Commonwealth.

In 1973 Ireland joined the **European Economic Community**, a move which both opened doors overseas and gave a huge boost to the economy.

Sweeping – some would say excessive – development changed the face of Dublin in the 1960s and 1970s. Much of the city's slum housing was demolished, and much of Georgian Dublin was sacrificed to the bulldozer, to be replaced by ugly and characterless office blocks and shopping complexes. This process slowed in the 1980s, and recent development has been more sensitive to the need to preserve the best of Dublin's architectural heritage.

GOVERNMENT AND ECONOMY

Ireland is a democratically governed republic, with a two-chamber parliament, the **Dail**. The head of state is the President. This post is largely ceremonial, but some presidents (including Ireland's first woman president, Mary Robinson, elected in 1990) have successfully influenced the government on key issues.

Below: *Leinster House, seat of the Irish parliament.*
Opposite: *Orange, white and green, Ireland's national colours.*

Day to day political power is held by the Taoiseach (prime minister).

The Dail is elected by a system of proportional representation which apportions votes very fairly, but frequently leaves no one party with a commanding majority. As a result, Irish politics are characterised by minority governments, coalitions, and the art of the political deal.

Dublin's figurehead is the Lord Mayor, but the running of the city is in the hands of a city manager appointed directly by the national government.

Agriculture and fishing are still very important sectors of the Irish economy, but light manufacturing, electronics, the service sector and tourism all generate substantial proportions of gross national product.

MARY ROBINSON

Mary Robinson was elected Ireland's first woman president in 1990. Previously, the presidency had been seen as a mainly ceremonial post, but Mrs Robinson, a Labour Party senator and a distinguished lawyer, made it much more active, campaigning strongly on women's rights. She has a history of campaigning, and during the 1970s was one of the leaders of the movement to block the Dublin Corporation's unpopular plans for a massive office project at Wood Quay, where Dublin's oldest Viking streets had been unearthed.

Until recently, Ireland was one of the European Union's least prosperous economies and Dublin one of its most depressed capitals, but since the early 1990s the city has undergone a striking financial renaissance. Government initiatives to develop the financial services sector and attract international banking and insurance companies to locate in Dublin have been outstandingly successful, aided by a young and energetic workforce. Lack of jobs for school leavers has encouraged a high proportion of young Dubliners to stay on in further education, creating a pool of well-educated potential employees. Remarkably, by the mid 1990s the national economy had become the fastest-growing in Europe, outstripping the EU's major economies. A new sense of prosperity and self-confidence is reflected in Dublin today, where higher disposable incomes have helped to fuel a boom in trendy new restaurants, bars, clubs and shops. The downside of this is a widening gap between haves and have-nots. The rate of unemployment, especially among young people, is still one of the highest in Europe and not much of the 1990s financial services boom has trickled down to the deprived suburbs of Dublin's north side.

WHO'S WHO

Two major parties – Fianna Fail, founded in 1926 by former opponents of the 1922 partition treaty, and Fine Gael, founded in 1933 and the descendant of Cumann na nGaedheal, the first pre-treaty party – have dominated Dublin politics since independence. Fianna Fail is more conservative on many issues, but the two are not clearly divided along traditional left-right lines. Left of both stands the Labour Party, which has sometimes allied with Fine Gael in coalition governments. On the extreme nationalist wing of Irish politics is Sinn Fein, closely identified with the Provisional IRA and its armed struggle in the North. The first Green Party member of the Dail was elected in 1989.

TRUE DUBS

Unlike many European cities,
Dublin's population has
grown and changed in the
last half-century. Bright city
lights and the prospect of
employment attract many
young people from rural
Ireland to the capital, and
native Dubliners may sometimes be heard muttering
about being swamped by
incomers. If you were born
and raised in Dublin you are a
'*Dub*', and in your own eyes
infinitely more sophisticated
than any '*culchie*', or incomer
from the countryside.

Many Dubliners go abroad – to the UK, other
European Union countries (much of the administration
of the European Commission in Brussels seems to be in
Irish hands) and to the USA – in search of better-paid
jobs. Earnings repatriated by these expatriates are an
important source of foreign exchange. The cost of living
is relatively high, partly because of high rates of direct
and indirect taxation on a small tax base and partly
because Ireland needs to import most of its raw materials, essential fuels, and many manufactured products.

THE PEOPLE

Dubliners are by reputation quick-witted, loquacious
and sociable, and certainly anyone sitting alone in a
Dublin pub is unlikely to remain for long without
falling into conversation with someone. Like most
people who like to talk, the typical Dubliner is rarely
without an opinion on any subject under the sun.

Above all, as any frequent visitor will tell you, Dublin
is a city in which it is fatally easy to be seduced into feeling like an insider. All you need to do to put your finger
on Dublin's pulse is to allow yourself to be drawn into
conversation. This is not difficult. Dubliners of every gen-

Below: *Enjoying a pint in
the Stag's Head.*

der and generation and of whatever political persuasion
are free with their opinions and eager to share whatever
titbits of gossip they may have
picked up recently.

Information travels faster on
the city's bar-and-coffee-house
grapevine than it does on TV
or radio, and every Dubliner
considers it a God-given right
to add his or her own opinion
to any choice piece of news,
whether it deals with the fortunes of the Irish football team,
the latest piece of government
legislation, or the local contender's chances of winning
this year's Song for Europe

contest. The average Dubliner feels equally qualified to hold strong opinions on matters not just of local but of world importance. But beware of venturing your own opinion: sticking your neck out exposes you to a barrage of the mordant sarcasm which is a central weapon in the Dubliners' conversational arsenal.

But Dubliners are also good listeners, with a healthy curiosity about life elsewhere. Many of the Dubliners you will meet may have worked abroad – in Britain, Europe, the USA or further afield – and the presence of large communities of Irish descent in many American and Australian cities means the Irish feel a special affinity for those countries. A high birth rate since World War II has given Ireland one of the youngest populations in the European Union, with more under-25s than any other EU country, a factor that gives Dublin social life much of its youthful energy.

Above: *Dublin has become a young and stylish city.*

You should also be aware that Dublin, like most big cities, has its own deep social and economic divisions. In some ways these have been deepened by the economic changes of the 1980s, when the city's economy plunged into the doldrums, and the 1990s, when it began to recover. In the drab state housing estates north and west of the city, unemployment is extremely high. Many young people growing up here view the future without hope and feel no connection with the bright lights and vibrant future of the more prosperous city centre and the wealthier suburbs of south Dublin.

Isolated on the fringes of Europe in the first decades after independence, modern Dublin is now a vibrant, forward-looking European capital.

Language

English – albeit a distinctively Irish form of it – is Ireland's first language. Irish, sometimes also called Gaelic, became neglected under British rule, when its use was discouraged and sometimes banned.

DUBLIN SLANG

Dublin has its own city argot, with a plethora of slang unfamiliar to speakers of other variants of English. For example, a whole vocabulary dedicated to describing various stages of inebriation, from '*dankey*' (mildly drunk) through '*fluthered*' (seriously drunk), '*jarred*' (very drunk), '*langers*' (very drunk indeed) to '*scuttered*' (falling down drunk). Pick up an entirely new vocabulary as you go along.

CHURCH SERVICES

Dublin is overwhelmingly Catholic, though its two Cathedrals belong to the Anglican Church of Ireland. Masses are usually held between 08:00 and 13:00 and between 17:00 and 19:00. Latin Mass is celebrated at the St Mary's Pro-Cathedral at 11:00 every Sunday. Most other faiths also have places of worship in the city.

Irish language is a Celtic tongue closely linked to Scots Gaelic, Welsh and Breton. Reviving its use was a central priority of the nationalist movement and of the Free State government after independence. Irish is taught in schools, and one in three Irish people now claim to speak it in addition to English (compared with one in four 30 years ago). There are, however, no monoglot Irish speakers, and in Dublin anyone you meet is more likely to speak the city's own lively dialect of English than to communicate in Ireland's older tongue. Nevertheless, official documents and titles, road signs and some place names are in both Irish and English.

Religion

Catholicism and Irish nationalism have been inextricably bound together for four centuries, and since independence the Catholic church has played an extremely active part in Irish political life.

Virtually all the Republic's citizens are Catholics, and the hierarchy of the Catholic church in Ireland is traditionally extremely conservative, with no inhibitions about mobilising its priests to influence secular politics from the pulpit. Ireland's political system, which frequently leaves the party in power with a marginal majority or governing in coalition, has also meant political parties of all persuasions are reluctant to cross the Church. Over the last three decades, the Church, in alliance with conservative politicians, has fought a determined campaign against such evils as sex education in schools, contraception, abortion and divorce. As a result, contraception and abortion remained illegal until recently and homosexuality ceased to be a crime only in 1993. A referendum on divorce in 1986 saw the Church mobilise its full influence and resulted in a 63% vote against changing the constitution to permit couples to divorce. In 1995, a second referendum overturned this decision with a very narrow majority voting to allow divorce.

Below: *Statues of the Madonna guard devout Dublin homes.*

Sport and Leisure

Dubliners take a lively interest in sport, but neither home-grown Irish games like hurling and Gaelic football, nor imported international sports such as soccer or rugby, arouse obsessive interest. Gaelic football – a fast-moving contact sport like a mixture of soccer and rugby but with fewer rules than either – stirs few passions in urban Dublin. Nor does hurling, despite its ancient Irish roots. And although a rugby international at Lansdowne Road guarantees a good turn-out, Dubliners are likely to be outnumbered by pilgrims from the rest of the country and – since the Irish team comprises players from the North as well as the Republic – even from Northern Ireland.

Soccer arouses more enthusiastic support, though oddly enough most Dubliners would sooner debate the relative merits of leading English and Scottish clubs (many of which have Irish players) than follow the fortunes of a local soccer team. Perhaps this has something to do with the weather. Many Dublin soccer fans feel that watching a tense confrontation between Manchester United and Liverpool on television in the comfort of a cosy bar, pint of Guinness in hand, is much more appealing than watching Shamrock Rovers, the city's biggest club, from the stands on a chilly winter's day.

> ### GAELIC FOOTBALL
>
> Gaelic football is played with a round ball like a soccer ball, but, as in rugby, players are allowed to handle and run with the ball. This is an exciting and highly physical game, but is not as popular in urban Dublin as in the rest of Ireland. Indeed, most Dublin sports fans are far more interested in the fortunes of English and Scottish soccer teams like Manchester United, Liverpool, and Glasgow Celtic – many of which field Irish players – than in the national game.

Below: *The Royal Dublin Golf Course, Dollymount.*

> ### HURLING
>
> Hurling looks lethal. A distant relative of hockey, the sport is played with a paddle-like wooden stick with the broad head of which the ball may be caught, balanced, or hurled with great force. Like Gaelic football, hurling is a very fast-moving game, and in the flurry of whirling sticks it seems amazing that any player can emerge unscathed. It is also a game with a long history – Irish legends and the earliest written and pictorial sources show that a version was being played in the earliest Celtic times.

Above: *Sailing on the Liffey estuary.*
Below: *Horses and riding are part of Dublin's way of life and are celebrated annually at the Dublin Horse Show.*
Opposite: *James Joyce, now idolised, had to leave Dublin to make his name.*

On the other hand, many Dubliners will happily join the flock of soccer pilgrims who follow the national team's fortunes abroad on the rare occasions that Ireland qualifies beyond the early stages of international championships like the World Cup.

Golf has a strong following, and there are several fine golf courses within easy reach of the city centre. With the Irish Sea on Dublin's doorstep, yachting is also popular with better-off Dubliners. Though this rich man's sport is out of the reach of most, gleaming flotillas moored at the Howth and Dun Laoighaire marinas testify to the prosperity of Dublin's southern suburbs.

But if each of these sports has its audience, a near-religious devotion to horses and every sport involving them unites Dubliners of all ages and classes, from the north side corporation flats to the posh villas of Howth and the southern suburbs. The week of the Dublin Horse Show, held in the Ballsbridge exhibition grounds of the Royal Dublin Society each August, may be the high point of the equestrian year, but every weekend the city racecourses at Phoenix Park and Leopardstown pack in the punters, and literally millions of pounds can change hands in bets. When a major racing event is on the pub TV, only a brave or foolish man would even attempt to change channels to watch any lesser sport.

Art and Culture

There are many art galleries in Dublin for visitors to enjoy, exhibiting works from all periods. These include the **National Gallery of Ireland**, The **National Portrait Gallery** and the **Irish Museum of Modern Art**.

Architecture

Typical design elements of Dublin's surviving Georgian townhouses include arched fanlight windows above each front door – often with elegant tracery – sash windows with square panes, and ornamental iron balconies outside the first floor windows. Top floor windows are always smaller than those below. While the wealthiest aristocrats built their mansions in stone, Dublin's terraced houses are usually faced in red brick, and interiors are often graced by delicate ornamental plaster ceilings and friezes.

Literary Dublin

Words and music are part of the Irish soul, and few cities have such rich literary connections as Dublin, from **Jonathan Swift** in the 18th century to **Oscar Wilde** in the 19th, **James Joyce**

THE MALTON TRAIL

The 18th-century artist **James Malton** recorded the elegance of Georgian Dublin in a series of beautifully-etched aquatints of its loveliest buildings. The Malton Trail, starting at Trinity College, leads you around those which survive. Each building bears a panel showing Malton's vision of it, together with its history. The walk takes around two hours. Dublin Tourism has also produced a selection of walking guides for visitors with a special interest in aspects of the city, including Georgian Trail, an Old City Trail, Rock and Roll Trail and Cultural Trail.

DUBLIN'S FAMOUS PUBS

Dublin's famous pubs are close to the city's heart and repositories of Dublin tradition, folklore and humour, where porter, whiskey and talk flow in equal quantities. The finest have preserved many of their original 19th-century fittings and furnishings, with magnificent carved mahogany bars, marble counters and gilt and frosted mirrors. Dublin bars have been a refuge and an inspiration for a literary pantheon that includes James Joyce, Flann O'Brien, Brendan Behan, Sean O'Casey and many more.

IN SESSION

The Gaelic word 'seisiuin' (session) has a special meaning. Originally an impromptu evening of music and song, starting in a bar and perhaps finishing in the early hours of the morning, sessions (more or less authentic depending on the mix of Dubliners and tourists) are organized regularly by many Dublin pubs and hotels. Some of the most authentic traditional music can be heard at sessions organised by Comhaltas Ceoltori Eireann, the Irish cultural association, which has nightly music sessions at its headquarters at Belgrave Square, Monkstown, Co. Dublin in summer and every Friday night year-round. For information, tel: (01) 280-0295.

in the early 20th century and – in the 1980s and 1990s – names like Nobel Prize-winning poet **Seamus Heaney**, Booker Prizewinner **Roddy Doyle** and playwright **Brian Friel**.

One of Dublin's best-loved landmarks is the Abbey Theatre, home of the National Theatre of Ireland. Founded in 1904 by a group which included the great Irish poet **William Butler Yeats**, the Abbey was to endow Dublin with a professional theatre company which would break the English stranglehold on Irish culture and provide a stage for Irish actors to perform plays by Irish playwrights to an Irish audience. Among the authors whose work it fostered were **J M Synge**, whose *The Playboy of the Western World* got a hostile reception in 1907. **Sean O'Casey**, whose *The Plough and the Stars* was produced at the Abbey, was, like Synge, accused of slandering the Irish people in a play which demythologised the Easter Rising, in which O'Casey had taken part. Contemporary Dublin writers include Roddy Doyle, whose trilogy of stories (two of which have been filmed) centres on the chaotic life of a working-class family on Dublin's Northside.

Music

Music and song are everywhere in Dublin, with folk and contemporary music far outweighing the classics. Traditional Irish music began its revival in the 1960s, and its following grew hugely in the 1970s, when bands like Planxty and later the Bothy Band began to fuse its rhythms and melodies with newer arrangements and instruments to create a new, yet still distinctively Irish sound. In the 1980s and 90s, Dublin-based musicians have been leading players in the world music movement, combining Irish traditions with influences from Europe and the

Irish folk music underwent a renaissance in the 1970s and 80s and is alive and kicking today in Dublin's pubs and other music venues. Some venues cater to visitors, with bands belting out well-loved ballads. Others are for purists intent on revitalizing traditional forms, and a growing number present musicians playing a fusion of Irish music with rock or with folk music from around the world. Best-loved of traditional Irish instruments include the harp, which has been played in Ireland since the earliest times – a 14th-century harp is on show in Trinity College – and the Uillean pipes, Ireland's version of the bagpipes.

Americas and even further afield. Traditional music is perhaps healthier today than it has been for centuries, yet among purists there is concern for its future, under siege from a myriad different musical styles which threaten to swamp it. At the same time, the new generation of young Dubliners are assailed by more musical choice, both in the city's dozens of live music venues and from satellite and cable TV, cassette and CD, than ever before. Europe's most youthful capital continues to prove itself a mine of musical talent, with new-established rock superstars such as U2, Sinead O'Connor and more recently the Cranberries remaining close to their Irish roots, while less well known internationally, but well-loved at home, are folk musicians like The Dubliners, The Chieftains, Clannad, and singer-satirist Christy Moore.

Classical music lovers are less well served. The city's only purpose-built venue for classical music is the National Concert Hall, home of the National Symphony Orchestra. The National Concert Hall also plays host to a variety of visiting orchestras and an even larger cast of big-name crooners and middle-aged crowd-pleasers.

Above: *The National Concert Hall hosts visiting orchestras and stars.*
Opposite: *Some of Dublin's many street musicians.*

While the 1950s and 60s were the decades of traditional or semi-traditional music in Dublin, led by bands like **The Dubliners**, the 70s and 80s saw a rock music explosion, powered by Dublin's youthful energy and led first by **Bob Geldof** and the **Boomtown Rats**. In the 1980s **U2** and **Sinead O'Connor** soared to world prominence, followed by the **Cranberries** in the 90s.

Above: *Director-star Mel Gibson marshals extras for* Braveheart, *the 'Scottish' epic shot in Ireland.*

Film

Movies have always had a big following in Dublin. In fact, Dubliners visit the cinema more frequently than any other Europeans, partly because of the very limited choice and staid, censored programming on television in Ireland. The advent of video and satellite TV today challenges cinema's popularity, but Ireland produces strong home-grown film talent of world-class quality – think of director **Neil Jordan**, for example, whose films *The Crying Game* and *Michael Collins* won international acclaim, or of top film actors like **Gabriel Byrne** and **Liam Neeson**. Despite government moves to cut tax relief which attracted international productions including **Mel Gibson's** multiple Oscar-winning *Braveheart* – shot mostly in Ireland – the Irish film industry is worth some 190 million annually, and employs up to 2000 people. The Irish Film Centre in the rejuvenated and thriving Temple Bar district is always worth a visit, and frequently shows seasons of new and established

Irish film-makers. The annual Dublin Film Festival, usually held in March/April, was launched in the mid 1980s and is now an established event. For cinema fans, it is the ideal time to visit the city, with more than 140 feature films from all over the world being shown at venues across the city.

Food and Drink

Traditional Irish food is best described as hearty, heavy on calories and usually based on beef or mutton, with plenty of

Above: *Irish cuisine is hearty and filling.*
Opposite bottom: *Delivering Guinness.*

root vegetables such as potatoes, carrots, onions and turnips, typified by dishes like Irish stew, Bacon and Cabbage, Champ (mashed potatoes with butter and onions) and Dublin Coddle (a comforting plate of sausages, bacon, onions and potatoes). Irish cheeses worth trying include Carrigaline and St Killian. Baked goods are excellent: the traditional fruit loaf known as Barm brack, soda bread and Guinness cake, a fruitcake flavoured with the traditional black brew. Irish scones are also very popular.

Since the 1980s Irish cooking has changed with the times. Irish chefs have created a new style of cookery, based on Ireland's superb local produce – fine beef and lamb, superb dairy products and terrific seafood from the Atlantic coasts – often cooked in a style strongly influenced by nouvelle cuisine. Partly, this revolution in Irish cooking has been part and parcel of the 'Europeanisation' of Ireland. Membership of the European Union has made it easier for young Dubliners to travel and work abroad, and many of them have

---

LIFFEY SALMON

If you venture up the Liffey Valley on New Year's morning, you'll see dozens of hopeful anglers flogging the water in the contest to take the first river salmon of the new year. Favoured spots are the cleaner upper stretches of the river, but plenty of optimistic souls try their luck in the Dublin suburbs. Dublin's top restaurants pay dearly for the year's first salmon, and there is something of a race to get the catch back into town first.

Above left: *Murphy's stout rivals the better-known Guinness.*

IRISH WHISKEY

Christian monks brought distillation to Ireland in the 6th century AD, perhaps from the Arab world, where stills were used to make perfume. Feeling the need of a warming dram in the chilly climate of their new Atlantic home, they turned to making *uisce beatha* (pronounced isk'ke-ba'ha) – the Water of Life. Ireland has never been the same since. Irish whiskeys are made from malted barley which is dried in a closed kiln, not over an open fire like the barley which goes to make Scotch, and as a result the Irish version lacks the distinctive smoky flavour of Scotch whisky.

---

chosen to work in the catering industry. Trained by French and Italian chefs, some have returned home to revitalise the Dublin restaurant world.

Diners in Dublin have never had such a wide range of gourmet options, and the list of the capital's fine restaurants gets longer every year. Hoteliers and restaurateurs get every encouragement from the Irish Food Board, which uses establishments throughout the country to showcase what it claims are the best raw materials in the world. The Restaurants Association of Ireland and the Irish Tourist Board produce an annual guide, *Dining in Ireland*, which lists more than 400 Irish restaurants – over 80 of them in central Dublin and more than 50 in the outskirts of the city. They include small family-run bar-restaurants, pubs and five-star establishments serving everything from the latest trendy Pacific and Asian cuisine to stick-to-the-ribs Irish home cooking. Speciality game and seafood restaurants are also prominent on the Dublin diner's map.

Dublin is the home of Guinness, the creamy dark stout or porter which is Ireland's national drink. There are other porters – such as McCaffrey's, Beamish's and

Murphy's – but it is Guinness which rules the roost, fuelling many a high-flown literary conversation. Guinness is exported worldwide and brewed under license in many parts of the world, but as any Dubliner will tell you, it is not the real thing unless it has been brewed from the water of the River Liffey.

Irish whiskey (spelt with an 'e'), though not as widely famed as the Scotch stuff, in fact has a longer pedigree, for Irish monks are said to have discovered how to brew '*uisce beatha*' (the water of life) some centuries before the art was known in Scotland. Probably the best-known brand is Jameson's, with Paddy a close second and Bushmills – distilled in Northern Ireland but popular in the south too – another favourite. Irish whiskeys generally taste a little sweeter and, say connoisseurs, are smoother than equivalent Scotch whiskies.

Though Ireland is not a wine-producing country, excellent wines are imported from European wine-producing countries and elsewhere and Dublin has plenty of pleasant wine bars. Wine, however, tends to be relatively expensive compared to beers and whiskeys.

> **SMOKING BAN**
>
> Since 1 January 1996, smoking has been banned in Dublin taxis, hairdressing salons, crèches, playschools, doctors' and dentists' waiting rooms, financial institutions and pharmacies, as well as in bowling alleys and bingo halls. The next step, government ministers hinted, could be to forbid smoking even in the city's hundreds of bars, spelling an end to the uniquely foggy atmosphere of the quintessential Irish drinking establishment.

Opposite top right: *Enjoy Irish food in any of the city's plentiful restaurants.* **Below:** *One of Dublin's scores of bars.*

2
South Bank of the Liffey

Immediately south of the River Liffey is Dublin's oldest district. The heart of the city is studded with historic buildings from every era of Dublin's past, some of them dating from the very foundation of the city by the Norsemen in the 10th century. Along the south bank of the Liffey, a series of riverside streets bear names which are reminders of Dublin's merchant past – Victoria Quay, Ushers Quay, Merchants Quay, Wellington Quay, Aston Quay, Burgh Quay, George's Quay and City Quay. Merchant shipping no longer sails up the Liffey to load and unload right in the heart of the city, but in Dublin's 18th-century heyday this waterfront bristled with masts.

Today, office buildings line the river and dominate many of the historic squares of south Dublin, but immediately south of the river the restored Temple Bar district preserves a block of old cobbled streets and historic buildings. Eight bridges cross the Liffey in the city centre.

Liffey Bridge (Ha'penny Bridge) *

Named Wellington Bridge in honour of the Irish-born Duke of Wellington when it was built in 1816, this elegant footbridge crosses the Liffey between Merchants Arch on the south bank and Liffey Street on the north. It was one of the first cast-iron bridges. Though renamed after independence, it has in fact always been known as Ha'penny Bridge from the halfpenny toll which was originally charged to cross it. Crossing the bridge now costs nothing and offers a fine view of the Liffey and of the buildings along its banks.

DON'T MISS

*** Christ Church Cathedral: Dramatic medieval building with a fascinating crypt and tombstones.
*** Trinity College: Gracious 400-year-old building in landscaped grounds. Fine collection of historic books.
** Dublin Castle: The heart of medieval Dublin. Finely restored interiors and church.
* Dublinia: Purpose-built heritage centre recreates life in medieval Dublin.

Opposite: *The elegant campus of Trinity College.*

South of the Liffey

O'Connell Bridge *

Built in 1790, this wide stone bridge is the main cross-river traffic artery in the city centre and a landmark in its own right, with three elegantly-arched spans linking the two banks of the River Liffey. Part of the city planners' grand design for 18th- and 19th-century Dublin, the bridge was widened in 1880 and is almost as broad as it is long, carrying 10 lanes of traffic. Originally named Carlisle Bridge, it was renamed after independence in honour of James O'Connell, one of the martyred leaders of the 1916 Easter Rising.

From O'Connell Bridge, the broad thoroughfare of Westmoreland Street leads from the south bank to Trinity College and the Bank of Ireland, two of Dublin's most important historic buildings. A statue of Thomas Moore, the 19th-century romantic poet stands at the junction with College Street, and at the corner of Nassau Street, at the south end of Westmoreland Street, is a pavement plaque with a quotation from James Joyce's *Ulysses*.

TRINITY COLLEGE ***

The oldest and grandest university in Ireland, Trinity College is a gracious complex of buildings on a beautiful 40-acre site just south of the O'Connell Street Bridge and recently celebrated its 400th anniversary in 1992. Founded by Queen Elizabeth I in 1592, the College is now the home of the University of Ireland. Buildings on the campus, with its cobbled squares, shady trees and manicured lawns, date from as early as the 17th century, with many additions ranging from every era of Dublin's past.

Trinity Chapel *

The multi-denominational chapel, recently restored, stands on the cobbled Front Square beneath a 30m (100ft) Italianate bell-tower built in 1853 on the site of an early medieval monastery church. In sharp contrast to the older buildings around it is the somewhat bunker-like concrete form of the Berkeley Library, built in 1967 and claimed to be one of Ireland's outstanding modern buildings. It is named after the theologian and philosopher **Bishop George Berkeley** (1685–1753).

Graduates of Trinity include the 18th-century orator and politician **Edmund Burke**, the writer **Oliver Goldsmith**, satirist **Jonathan Swift** (author of *Gulliver's Travels*), playwright **Oscar Wilde**, and **Bram Stoker**, creator of Dracula. Goldsmith and Burke are honoured by statues in the campus grounds. Trinity excluded Catholics until 1873 and remained overwhelmingly Protestant until the 1960s, partly because the conservative Catholic church did its best to deter Catholic families from sending their children to a non-Catholic establishment. American author **J P Donleavy**, many of whose books are set in Dublin, made Trinity the backdrop for humorous and amatory escapades in novels such as *The Ginger Man* and *The Beastly Beatitudes of Balthazar B.*

THOMAS MOORE

One of Ireland's best-loved 19th-century poets and lyricists, Thomas Moore (1779–1852) was educated at Trinity College, Dublin and travelled widely in the United States and in Europe. He was the author of many poems and airs inspired by his native land, the best known of which are contained in the collection of Irish Melodies he published between 1807 and 1834. He was a close friend of Lord Byron, whose memoirs he was given to publish but later found so shocking that he destroyed them instead.

Below: *Trinity's bell-tower dates from 1853.*

Above: *A rich academic heritage has been built up at Trinity College.*
Below: *Trinity's Long Room Library is the finest in Ireland.*

Trinity College Colonnades *

Treasures displayed in the College's Colonnades gallery include the magnificent **Book of Kells**, the centrepiece of a special exhibition which opened in 1996 and is scheduled to run until 1999. This beautifully illuminated manuscript version of the four gospels dates from the 8th century and is one of the oldest surviving documents from Western Europe in the Christian era. The richly ornamented text is decorated with complex Celtic abstract designs and minutely detailed figures of fantastic creatures and figures. Illuminated manuscripts from the ancient monasteries of Durrow and Armagh are also on display along with one of the earliest Irish harps. Trinity's Long Room, the finest library in Ireland, houses more than 200,000 antiquarian volumes. Open Monday–Saturday 09:30–17:30, Sunday 12:00–17:00.

The Dublin Experience **

Trinity also houses The Dublin Experience, a striking audiovisual show which tells the story of Dublin and the Dubliners from the earliest times to the present day. It's a great introduction to the city and should not be missed. Open 22 May–29 September, daily 10:00–17:00.

BLUE PLAQUES

Throughout Dublin, blue wall plaques mark the homes or birthplaces of the scores of famous men and women who were born in the city or made it their home. There are more than 40 of them, from rock star **Bob Geldof** to poet **W B Yeats**. Not all of these renowned residents of Dublin are Irish – their ranks include quantum physicist **Erwin Schroedinger**, philosopher **Ludwig Wittgenstein**, composer **George Frederick Handel**, and **Guglielmo Marconi**, inventor of wireless radio.

BANK OF IRELAND (OLD IRISH PARLIAMENT) ★★★

Constructed in 1729 as the seat of the Irish Parliament, this elegant and striking building was the world's first purpose-built parliament house. It is now headquarters to the Bank of Ireland, which purchased it when the parliament ceased to exist and had it rebuilt by Francis Johnston, the architect responsible for many of Georgian Dublin's finest buildings. It housed the Protestant-dominated parliament until the Act of Union of 1800, which united the parliaments of Britain and Ireland.

It is sometimes claimed that the Irish Parliament is the only parliamentary body to have voted for its own abolition, but in fact the Scottish Parliament had done exactly the same in 1707, when it passed the Act of Union uniting Scotland with England to create the United Kingdom.

Above: *The Georgian portico of the Bank of Ireland.*

The whole front of the building, with its elegantly-pillared classical porticos, is 'blind': it was built without windows to protect the parliament from outside distractions and perhaps – given Dublin's occasionally turbulent history – to give the members of parliament better protection in times of civic unrest. Within, the most dazzling room is the chamber in which the Irish House of Lords, the upper house of the parliament, once sat. Panelled and decorated in Irish oak, this splendid hall is decorated with 18th-century tapestries. A glittering 18th-century chandelier made of more than 1200 pieces of cut crystal hangs from the ceiling and among the exhibits is the magnificent silver-gilt mace which was the symbol of the parliament. Open Monday–Friday 10:00–16:00, Thursday 10:00–17:00. Guided tours Tuesday at 10:30, 11:30, 13:45.

CITY WALLS

Though Dublin was ringed by a system of fortifications built first by the Vikings and extended by the Norman conquerors, virtually nothing remains of its medieval ramparts, which in the early 13th century stretched for almost 3km (2 miles). Documents dating from the late 16th century give detailed descriptions of the battlements, gates and defensive turrets, and a line of granite markers around the city centre marks where the walls once stood.

The rebirth of the old Temple Bar district as Dublin's 'Cultural Quarter' signalled a welcome reappraisal by the city's planners, speculators and managers, who in the 1960s and 70s presided over the wholesale destruction of much of Georgian Dublin in favour of unattractive modern commercial buildings, new roads and car parks. The successful revitalization of Temple Bar has given new hope for urban renewal, and pedestrianization of key shopping streets heralds a new awareness of the value of the city's older buildings.

Above: *The Temple Bar district is Dublin's 'Cultural Quarter'.*
Below: *Crown Alley in Temple Bar.*

TEMPLE BAR ★★★

The riverside Temple Bar district, recently reborn as Dublin's 'Cultural Quarter' on the south bank of the Liffey between Wellington Quay and Dame Street, is a block of cobbled streets laid out in the 18th century which has escaped demolition and redevelopment. Under an urban renewal project, launched in 1991 and scheduled for completion in 1996, its two-century-old buildings are being restored and the streets are being pedestrianized to create an attractive shopping and entertainment district full of innovative small art galleries, imaginative and colourful shops and the best choice of restaurants in Dublin. Temple Bar has also become a nightlife centre, with lots of theatres, cinemas, nightclubs and pubs.

Highlights of the Temple Bar district include the **Irish Film Centre**, with two cinemas showing a programme of Irish films, and **The Ark**, a children's cultural centre with a programme of videos and events aimed at bringing Irish culture to life for younger visitors. Both are on Eustace Street, in the heart of Temple Bar. The Temple Bar Information Centre (Curved Street/Eustace Street) is open from June–August weekdays 09:00–19:00, Saturday 11:00–19:00, Sunday 12:00–18:00, September–May weekdays 09:30–18:00, Saturday 12:00–18:00.

DUBLIN CASTLE ***

One of Dublin's oldest buildings, the castle has been added to and altered over centuries and is an attractive mixture of styles. The first stronghold on the site was a Viking fortress, but the oldest parts of the present building date from between 1208 and 1220. The castle's **Record Tower** is the most prominent part of the original 13th-century building, and the **Castle Yard** covers the area defended by the first set of ramparts. Recent excavations uncovered remnants of the even older Viking stronghold, part of which can now be seen in the medieval **Undercroft** section of the castle, which also houses a restaurant and heritage centre.

Dublin Castle was the seat of the British administration until independence, and its gracious State Apartments are used when Ireland holds the presidency of the European Union and on a variety of other state and diplomatic occasions. The huge **St Patrick's Hall**, with its high, vaulted ceiling, is the most imposing. Also within the castle walls is the **Church of the Most Holy Trinity**. Its superb interior has recently been renovated. Open Monday–Friday 10:00–12:15 and 14:00–17:00.

Above: *Dublin Castle is a mix of styles spanning many centuries.*
Below: *Inside the Dublin Castle.*

CHRIST CHURCH CATHEDRAL ***

The first cathedral on this site was built by the Christian Viking King **Sitric Silkenbeard**, but the city owes the present building to the Norman Earl of Pembroke, **Richard de Clare** ('Strongbow'), who ordered it built in 1169, immediately after his conquest of the city. A tomb in the south aisle carved with the form of an armoured knight is claimed to be that of Strongbow.

The cathedral was restored in the 16th century but by the mid 19th century it was again in need of massive restoration which began in 1871 when a number of Victorian Gothic features were also added. The oldest parts of the church are the south transept, which dates from around 1180, and the cavernous crypt below the cathedral which is supported by crudely built arches dating back to its Viking foundation.

The church contains many fine monumental sculptures and basses from the 16th to the 19th century, while the crypt's collection of relics includes the old punishment stocks of the Christ Church district and the candlesticks and tabernacle brought to Ireland by King James II when he fled England in 1689. Look out for the 'leaning wall' of the nave, which has been 46cm (18 in) off the vertical since 1562. Open daily 10:00–17:00.

In the churchyard in front of the cathedral are the ruins of the 13th-century **Chapter House**.

DUBLINIA *

This purpose built heritage centre developed by Dublin's Medieval Trust recreates everyday life in historic Dublin within a beautifully preserved building in the heart of old Dublin. Linked to Christ Church Cathedral by an elegant footbridge, the medieval maze brings four centuries of Dublin's past to life in a series of living tableaux and dioramas. High

points include life-size reconstructions of part of the 13th-century **Wood Quay** and the interior of a 15th-century **merchant's house**. Displays of genuine artefacts from the National Museum of Ireland give insight into work, commerce and leisure in medieval times.

A personal audio headset guides you through the exhibition, and a dramatic audiovisual presentation of sounds and sights of Dublin in the Great Hall, emphasising the city's historic links with Europe. Open April–30 September, daily 10:00–17:00, October–March, Monday–Saturday 11:00–16:00, Sunday 10:00–16:30.

Waterways Visitor Centre **

Two once-splendid canals, the Royal Canal in North Dublin and the Grand Canal in the south, link the Liffey with Ireland's river and canal systems. On Grand Canal Quay, overlooking the Grand Canal Basin where the canal meets the Liffey just a short distance to the east of the centre of the city, the new Waterways Visitor Centre houses a fascinating exhibition which introduces you to the story of Ireland's inland waterways. Attractions include an audiovisual presentation, working models of barges and canal locks, and a hands-on multi-media presentation which will delight younger visitors. Open June–September daily, 09:30–18:30, October–May, Wednesday–Sunday 12:30–17:00.

Above: *Dublinia recreates the city's medieval past.*
Opposite: *Christ Church Cathedral dates from the 12th century but was completely restored in the 19th.*

TOURISM

Dublin's tourism industry is in its infancy. Most visitors to Ireland are more interested in the stereotyped images of green hills, country villages, rivers and empty coastlines than in the frequently grimy and chaotic reality of the capital. The city gets less than half as many visitors each year as Edinburgh, and only 20% of the total visiting Amsterdam – both cities of comparable size and climate. On the positive side, there is a keen awareness in the private and public sector of the need to do more for visitors, and you will certainly not feel you are part of a tourist invasion.

3
St Stephen's Green and Surrounds

This area of south Dublin, between Trinity College and the southern sector of the Grand Canal which rings central Dublin, contains many of the city's best-preserved **Georgian buildings** and a number of fine **museums**.

The proximity of Trinity College to its large student population gives this part of town a youthful and slightly bohemian atmosphere, though it also contains some of Dublin's most elegant shops and restaurants.

GRAFTON STREET AND SURROUNDS

This street, which runs between Trinity College and St Stephen's Green, was an elegant residential area in the 18th century. Pedestrianized in the 1980s, it has Dublin's most expensive shops and during the summer is often populated with street musicians and entertainers. A number of interesting historic buildings and museums are to be found in the blocks on either side of Grafton Street.

St Ann's Church *

This elegant church just off Grafton Street was built in 1720 and has a neo-Romanesque façade which was added in 1868. Look for the special shelf beside the altar which was used to display bread before its distribution to the poor – the result of a bequest of an 18th-century aristocrat who left £13 a year to the poor of the parish to be distributed as bread each week.

St Ann's is well known for its lunchtime concerts. Open daily 09:00–18:00.

DON'T MISS

*** **St Patrick's Cathedral:** Dublin's second medieval cathedral.
*** **The Shaw Birthplace:** Recreates the Victorian world of the playwright's childhood.
*** **Newman House:** Two beautiful Georgian townhouses offer a recreation of the elegance and grace of wealthy 18th-century Dublin.
** **National Library:** A must for those in search of their Irish roots.
*** **Number Twenty Nine:** Elegantly-furnished 18th-century home opens a window onto a vanished past.

Opposite: *Beautiful St Stephen's Green.*

Royal Irish Academy ✶

The Royal Irish Academy is the principal Irish academic and historical society. The Academy's **library** of early and medieval Irish manuscripts (some more than 1000 years old) is one of the largest and finest in the world, though possibly of more interest to the specialist scholar than to the average visitor. Open Monday–Friday 09:30–17:30.

Dublin Civic Museum ✶✶

The Civic Museum, housed in what was once the City Assembly House where Dublin's municipal council met, is dedicated to the history of the city and portrays many aspects of Dublin's rich past from its earliest years through to the present day. Opened in 1953, it has a very wide-ranging collection, with artefacts, documents and displays ranging from relics of the Viking Era to a model of one of 19th-century Dublin's tramcars. The permanent collection includes sections on Dublin's streets and buildings, trade and industry, transport, political history, and maps and views of the city as it once was. Open Tuesday–Saturday 10:00–18:00, Sunday 11:00–14:00.

There are also fascinating temporary exhibitions several times each year.

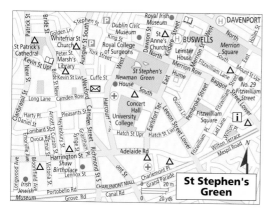

St Stephen's Green

WEST OF ST STEPHEN'S GREEN

St Patrick's Cathedral ✶✶

Dublin's second medieval cathedral stands on what is claimed to be the city's oldest Christian site. Ireland's patron saint reputedly baptized his converts to Christianity in a well located here. The first church on the spot was built in AD450, and replaced in 1191 by the

present building. Like Christ Church, it was badly neglected before being extensively restored in the 1860s, so what you now see – an attractive building in light-coloured limestone with a taller, slimmer tower than the rival Christ Church Cathedral – is a Victorian reinterpretation of the original Norman building. The West Tower, which was added in 1370, contains the largest carillon in Ireland.

Within the cathedral are Celtic tombstones, and the transepts are graced by the faded banners of Irish regiments. The most striking of the church's monuments is the painted representation of the Boyle dynasty, the Earls of Cork, placed in the church by Richard Boyle in the early 17th century. **Jonathan Swift**, author of *Gulliver's Travels*, was Dean of St Patrick's from 1713 to 1745. He is buried in the cathedral, and you can also see his pulpit, chair and writing desk and the scroll honouring him as a Freeman of the City. Other famous Irishmen buried in St Patrick's include Turlough O'Carolan, last of the great Irish bardic harpists, and Douglas Hyde, the Republic's first president.

Above: *Stained glass adds elegance to Bewley's Oriental Café.*

MAKING PEACE

Look out for the old wooden door in the south transept of St Patrick. The fist-sized hole roughly cut in it dates from 1492, when the Earls of Kildare and Ormonde and their bodyguards fell out and Ormonde was forced to take refuge in the chapter house. The hole was cut in the door so that the two turbulent noblemen might shake hands and make peace before again meeting face to face.

Right: *Marsh's Library is a treasury of antiquarian books and manuscripts.*
Opposite: *Figures of the Virgin and St Valentine in the Carmelite Church, Whitefriar Street.*

Like Christ Church Cathedral, St Patrick's belongs to the Anglican Church of Ireland. Ironically, this over-whelmingly Catholic city has no Roman Catholic cathedral, and its earliest Roman Catholic churches date from less than two centuries ago. Until the early 19th century, Catholics were not permitted to worship open-ly. Open Monday–Friday 09:00–18:00, Saturday 09:00–17:00, Sunday 10:00–16:30.

Marsh's Library *

This solid, well-proportioned red-brick building is Ireland's oldest public library. It was built in 1701 by Archbishop Narcissus Marsh (1638–1713) and contains 25,000 priceless antique books, manuscripts and maps. While the rare works of literature are of more interest to scholars than to casual visitors, the library's well-pre-served interior, with its lovely dark oak shelves, each adorned with carving and carved lettering, is worth seeing. Its curiosities include the three 'cages', cell-like wired alcoves in which scholars of rare books are locked while they read, as an anti-theft measure. Open Wednesday–Friday 10:00–12:45 and 14:00–17:00, Saturday 10:30–12:45, Monday 10:00–12:45 and 14:00–17:00.

WOODEN VIRGIN

On display in the northeast corner of Whitefriar Street Carmelite Church is a beauti-ful 16th-century statue of the Virgin Mary and child. Carved out of Flemish oak, it is believed to be the only known wooden statue to have escaped destruction during the Reformation and was previously property of St Mary's Abbey in north Dublin.

The Liberties

Just west of St Patrick's Cathedral, at the junction of Upper Kevin Street and Francis Street is the gateway to The Liberties. This district, outside the walls of the medieval city, was free of the restrictions on trade within the city.

Until the 1950s the Liberties remained an archetypal inner-city slum, its much-vaunted colour and character composed of equal parts of poverty, overcrowding, poor sanitation and barely-habitable housing. Most of the people who lived there then have been decanted to better-equipped but soulless housing estates on the city outskirts, while the homes which survive have been sanitized and beautified by their new owners, the well-off middle-class professionals of Dublin.

Today, Francis Street is a great place to browse for antiques and curios in the many antique shops, and the Friday and Saturday street market in Meath Street, parallel to Francis Street, is a good place to hunt for bargains, junk, and antique clothing.

> **THE FAIRY PEOPLE**
>
> *Daoine Sidhe*, or the Fairy People, are a popular part of Irish myth and folklore. Traditionally believed to be fallen angels who were banished from Heaven with Lucifer, but not bad enough to go to Hell, they are mischievous but not malevolent creatures who are quick to take umbrage but can easily be assuaged by leaving a bowl of milk outside your window overnight. The best known and most appealing is the leprechaun, who buries crocks of gold at the end of rainbows. The Fairy People are associated with the hawthorne and the whitethorn, both regarded as sacred trees in Irish myth, and bad luck is said to befall anyone who cuts one down.

Whitefriar Street Carmelite Church *

Begun in 1825, the church stands on the location of a 16th-century Carmelite Priory which was completely destroyed during the Reformation. Inside the Church is St Albert's Well, the water of which is said to have healing properties if used in conjunction with prayers on St Albert's Day (7 August) when a relic of the Sicilian saint is dipped in the well. The church also contains relics of St Valentine, whose remains were granted to the newly built church by Pope Gregory XVI in 1835. Prominent in the church is a life-sized oak figure of the Virgin, Our Lady of Dublin. Open Monday, Wednesday, Thursday, Friday 08:00–18:30, Saturday 08:00–19:00, Sunday 08:00–19:30.

Above: *George Bernard Shaw's birthplace recreates mid-19th-century bourgeois Dublin.*
Below: *The huge shopping centre at St Stephen's Green.*
Opposite: *Relaxing in the sun on beautiful St Stephen's Green.*

The Shaw Birthplace ★★★

The birthplace of George Bernard Shaw (1856–1950) was reopened as a visitor attraction in 1993. Decorated and furnished throughout in the authentic style of the mid-19th century, the interior brilliantly recreates the world of a Victorian middle-class Dublin family. In the scullery area a small informative display fills you in on the background of Shaw and his times, and you can also explore the stuffily furnished and decorated front parlour, the childrens' bedroom, upstairs drawing room and a tidy, peaceful Victorian back garden. Open May–October Monday–Saturday 10:00–17:00.

Irish Jewish Museum ★

Housed in a restored synagogue, this small museum has a collection of objects and documents relating to Jewish life in Dublin over the past two centuries. Dublin had a significant Jewish community from at least Norman times. Open April–September Tuesday, Thursday, Sunday 11:00– 15:30, October–March 10:30–14:30.

ST STEPHEN'S GREEN

Until the 17th century St Stephen's Green was open common land, but as Dublin expanded southward in the 17th century it was enclosed. During the 18th century, fashionable Georgian mansions and public buildings sprang up around it. Most of these have sadly fallen victim to the urban developer, but the few which remain are strikingly attractive.

In the centre of the Green are landscaped gardens, laid out around decorative ponds in 1880 as a public park and given to the city by **Sir Arthur Guinness** (first Baron Ardilaun, 1840–1915), grandson of the founder of the wealthy Guinness brewing dynasty. This part of Dublin owes much to the Guinnesses: **Sir Benjamin Guinness**, first baronet (1798–1868) consolidated the brewing empire, became Lord Mayor of Dublin in 1851, and restored St Patrick's Cathedral at a cost of £150,000. St Stephen's Green is a favourite summer picnic spot and refuge from the surrounding city street. Landmarks

---

DUBLIN WRITERS

Dublin today proudly claims as its own the likes of **W B Yeats**, **James Joyce** and **Samuel Beckett**, to name but a few of the famous literary men born in the city. Yet most of them couldn't wait to leave the place for more fertile territory – Shaw, Yeats and Wilde for London, Beckett for Paris and Joyce for first Paris, then Zurich. None of them seem to have had a good word to say for the place, but Dublin today – no longer a backwater but an exciting and cosmopolitan city – meets with greater approval.

within the park include a triumphal arch at the north-west gateway dedicated to the Dublin Fusiliers, and statues commemorating 18th-century patriot Wolfe Tone and playwright W B Yeats. Open June–30 September, Tuesday–Friday 10:00–16:30, Saturday 14:00–16:30, Sunday 11:00–14:00.

Newman House ★★★

Two beautiful Georgian townhouses, restored in 1989, offer the finest recreation of the elegance and grace of wealthy 18th-century Dublin. Open June–30 September Tuesday–Friday 10:00–16:30, Saturday 14:00–16:30, Sunday 11:00–14:00.

During the 19th century the buildings housed the Catholic University founded by Cardinal Newman. Among its students (from 1899 to 1902) was the author James Joyce and among its dons was the poet Gerald Manley Hopkins, who was professor of classics from 1884 to 1889. A guided tour puts the buildings in their historic context and helps to picture the lives of their inhabitants in the 18th century.

TRACING YOUR ROOTS

Many more people of Irish descent live overseas than in the Republic itself. If you are one of them, and are keen to trace your Irish roots, the best place to start is in Dublin's Kildare Street. The National Library (see opposite) with its huge collection of newspapers and magazines is a good place to look for clues to your ancestry, such as birth and wedding announcements, while next door at 2 Kildare Street the Irish Genealogical Office and State Heraldic Museum offers a consultancy service on ancestry tracing.

Royal College of Surgeons in Ireland ★★★

The jewel in the Green's Georgian crown and among the most outstanding Georgian buildings in Dublin is the Royal College of Surgeons, which stands at the northwest corner of the Green. This elegantly proportioned building dates from 1806 and was designed by the architect Edward Parke. During the bloody and abortive Easter Rising of 1916 it was seized by a handful of republican volunteers led by Countess Constance Marciewicz.

LIBRARIES AND MUSEUMS
National Library ★

For those in search of their Irish ancestry, this grand library just north of St Stephen's Green is the place to start. The library has an enormous archive, including

near-complete runs of every newspaper and magazine ever printed in Ireland and a huge reference section of books on every aspect of Ireland. The round entrance hall, with its colonnade and fine mosaic floor decorated with the signs of the zodiac, is often used for temporary exhibitions. Open Monday 10:00–21:00, Tuesday/ Wednesday 14:00–21:00, Thursday/Friday 10:00–17:00, Saturday 10:00–13:00.

Above: *The restored façade of Newman House.*
Opposite: *The gracious Georgian façade of the Royal College of Surgeons in Ireland.*

Heraldic Museum ★★

This fascinating little museum next to the National Library, with its displays of decorated shields, flags, coins and stamps claims to be the only one in the world dedicated to the vanishing science of heraldry. It was founded in 1911. Open Monday–Friday 10:00–12:30 and 14:00–16:30.

Leinster House **

Leinster House, now the seat of the **Oireachtais** (Irish Parliament), was built in 1745 for the Dukes of Leinster. In 1814 the mansion was bought by the Royal Dublin Society, an academic and literary association, and passed into the hands of the government on independence. The building's most impressive room is the Seanad (Senate) hall in the north wing, with a decorative stucco interior. Two of Dublin's largest museums stand on either side of Leinster House – the National Museum on its west side and the Natural History Museum to the east. Open Monday–Friday 09:00–17:00 when parliament is not in session.

National Museum of Ireland ***

If you are interested in the complicated and fascinating history of Ireland and its capital you should plan on spending half a day here.

The National Museum, set up in 1890, has a vast and far-reaching collection. Among its high points, and calculated to impress even the most blasé visitor, is the National Treasury, which includes the magnificently decorated **Ardagh Chalice** and the intricately worked golden **Tara Brooch** and **Cross of Cong**, priceless relics

of Ireland's early Christian era. **Ireland's Gold**, another breathtaking display, comprises gorgeously made gold artefacts found in Ireland's deep peat bogs, while a Prehistoric Ireland section sets this treasure in its everyday context. Also interesting, if less immediately awe-inspiring, are the collections of ceramics, Irish silverware, glassware, and scientific

instruments, while the *Ar Thoir na Saoirse* (the Road to Independence) is a useful introduction to the events of the struggle for Irish freedom from 1916 to 1921. Open Tuesday–Saturday 10:00–17:00, Sunday 14:00–17:00.

Above: *Typical Georgian architecture on Merrion Square has fortunately survived demolition.*
Opposite: *Built for 18th-century aristocrats, Leinster House is the seat of the Irish parliament.*

Natural History Museum *

Perhaps the most interesting single exhibit in the museum dedicated to Ireland's wildlife is the massive skeleton of the now-extinct giant Irish deer which roamed the island in prehistoric times until hunted to extinction by the earliest Stone Age settlers. Look out too for the skeletons of two whales found stranded on Ireland's Atlantic coast. The main displays on Irish wildlife are on the ground floor. Open Tuesday–Saturday 10:00–17:00, Sunday 14:00–17:00.

MERRION SQUARE

This Georgian square with its pretty park, a short distance northwest of St Stephen's Green, has seen many of Dublin's most famous literary and political figures come and go. Walk around the square looking out for wall plaques marking the birthplace of playwright Oscar Wilde at No 1; the home of writer and legislator Sir Jonah Barrington at No 42; lawyer and politician Daniel O'Connell's house at No 58; mystery writer Sheridan le Fanu's residence at No 70; and the home

Above: *Fitzwilliam Square is charmingly well-preserved.*

of famous Nobel prize-winning physicist **Erwin Schroedinger** at No 65. Poet **W B Yeats**, another of Dublin's Nobel winners, lived at both No 52 and No 82, though not simultaneously, and writer and painter George Russell had his studio at No 84. Just off Merrion Square, at Mornington House, 24 Upper Merrion Street, is the birthplace of Arthur, Viscount Wellesley, first Duke of Wellington.

National Gallery of Ireland ✶✶✶

Dublin is a city full of surprises, none more surprising than this unexpectedly fine collection of European art. Set up in 1854, the National Gallery is regarded as one of the best of its kind in Europe, with almost 2500 paintings, more than 5000 drawings and watercolours and more than 3000 prints. The collection includes works from virtually every school of European painting, including what is probably the world's best collection of Irish painters. Prominent among them are works by **Jack B Yeats**, late 19th-century Ireland's finest painter and brother of W B Yeats, the playwright. Also among the jewels of the National Gallery's collection of old masters are **Caravaggio**'s mighty *The Taking of Christ* and paintings by **Goya**, **Poussin** and **Gainsborough**. The gallery also hosts travelling exhibitions from leading international museums and collections.

A statue of **George Bernard Shaw** stands in front of the gallery; the playwright left one third of his entire estate to the National Gallery. Open Monday–Saturday 10:00–17:30, Thursday 10:00–20:30, Sunday 14:00–17:00. Guided tours are offered on Saturday 15:00 and Sunday 14:30, 15:15 and 16:00.

SCHROEDINGER'S CAT

Erwin Schroedinger, who lived and worked in Dublin between 1940 and 1956, devised the following illustration of quantum theory. Put a cat in a soundproofed box with a lethal mechanism triggered by the passage of a photon through a half-silvered mirror. The quantum probability of this happening is exactly one half, but there is no way of knowing what has happened until you open the box. Until then, two possibilities exist as waves; after, only one can exist. This is apparently central to quantum theory. Non-physicists may find comprehension is assisted by the timely application of several pints of Guinness.

FITZWILLIAM SQUARE

This elegant little Georgian square off Fitzwilliam Street, a short distance south of St Stephen's Green, is charmingly well-preserved. The earliest houses here date from 1714 and although the last buildings around the square were not completed until 1830 the continuity of style and detail is remarkable.

Number Twenty Nine ★★★

This elegantly furnished recreation of an 18th-century middle class household opens a window onto a vanished past. Owned by the National Museum of Ireland, the house is furnished and decorated as a typical home of a better-off Dublin family of the late 18th and early 19th century. The reception rooms on the ground floor are furnished with period pieces or finely made replicas, and the floor coverings, soft furnishings, paint and plaster are all in keeping with the period. The family bedrooms, nursery and playrooms with their 19th-century toys will fascinate children as well as adults. Open Tuesday–Saturday 10:00–17:00, Sunday 14:00–17:00.

Royal Hibernian Academy Gallagher Gallery ★

This modern building is a striking contrast to the stately National Gallery, but its exhibitions of contemporary Irish and foreign artists are well designed and always exciting. Open Monday–Saturday 11:00–17:00 and Sunday 14:00–17:00.

THE GRAND CANAL

Work on the Grand Canal, which sweeps in a 7km (4 mile) crescent through south Dublin to the Liffey, began in 1755. Though picturesque, it is no longer in commercial use, but there are some pleasant walks along its banks.

CANAL WALK

Start at the Butt Bridge, on St George's Quay, for an interesting walk along the south side of the Liffey with fine views of the stately Custom House on the opposite bank. Turn right onto the west bank of the Grand Canal Basin to visit the Waterways Visitor Information Centre, and continue round the arc of the Grand Canal. After about 1km (800 yd) a right turn on Lower Baggot Street will lead you back towards St Stephen's Green. Alternatively, a longer walk of around 4km (2½ miles) leads you to Richmond Street, where you can turn right to visit the Shaw Birthplace and return to the city centre.

Below: *A monument to 18th-century engineering, the Grand Canal.*

4
North of the Liffey

The city centre north of the Liffey has many of Dublin's most substantial public buildings, most of them dating from the late 18th and early 19th centuries, when this part of Dublin first became fashionable. Among the most influential men of the time was **Luke Gardiner**, first Viscount Mountjoy, who developed a new town of stylish mansions and squares. Many of these fine buildings fell into decay after the Act of Union in 1800, when Dublin's wealthiest and most influential families migrated to London. Many of north Dublin's museums and galleries are housed in painstakingly restored Georgian townhouses, with their typical fine stucco-work, wrought iron balconies and red-brick façades.

Today, this is perhaps the liveliest part of the city, with Dublin's busiest shopping streets, business districts and street markets. This area was the scene of heavy fighting between republican volunteers and British troops during the Easter Rising of 1916 and later between Free State government forces and hard-line republicans during the Civil War. The Custom House, just east of O'Connell Bridge, is a reminder that the north bank of the river was once busy with shipping, but the former docklands next to it have been rejuvenated as Dublin's new financial services centre.

DON'T MISS

*** **Dublin Writers Museum:** Literary museum in a grand 18th-century townhouse.
*** **James Joyce Cultural Centre:** Painstakingly restored shrine to the author of *Ulysses* and *Dubliners*.
*** **Irish Whiskey Corner:** Fascinating exhibition centre with model distillery and tasting centre.
** **St Michan's Church:** Historic church with 17th-century organ and crypt.

O'CONNELL STREET

The area is bisected by O'Connell Street, the widest and most important traffic artery through central Dublin. Running from north to south, it crosses the river by the O'Connell Bridge. Originally named Drogheda Street,

Opposite: *The recently restored Custom House façade is elaborately decorated.*

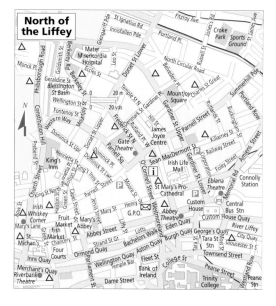

North of the Liffey

its plan was first laid out in the early 18th century, when substantial building north of the Liffey began in earnest. Later in the 18th century it was widened and rebuilt as a sweeping boulevard through the city. There was heavy fighting here during the Easter Rising of 1916 and in the Irish Civil War of 1922–23, and many buildings were severely damaged or demolished. Many of the street's more elegant buildings date from the 1920s, when there was extensive rebuilding. After independence, the street was renamed after Daniel O'Connell leader of the 19th-century Catholic emancipation movement.

General Post Office *

Designed by Francis Johnston and completed in 1818, the GPO has a graceful Ionic portico topped by three stone effigies of Mercury (the messenger of the gods), Fidelity and Hibernia (Ireland). The **Easter Rising** started here when a group of volunteers led by Padraic Pearse and James Connolly occupied the building on Easter Monday 1916 and held out under British bombardment for six days. The GPO building was severely damaged, and the present building is a reconstruction. In the main hall stands a memorial to the dead of the Easter Rising, symbolized by the dying hero Cuchulainn, one of the mighty warriors of Irish legend. Open Monday–Friday 08:30–17:00, Saturday 08:30–13:00.

MOORE STREET AND HENRY STREET

Running parallel to O'Connell Street, one block to the west, is Moore Street, central Dublin's main **produce market**. Open daily except Sunday, it is full of bustle, especially in the mornings. Fruit and vegetable traders sell their wares from numbered pitches, usually with a good deal of cheerful shouting – this is a fine place to hear Dublin's peculiar vernacular at its most incomprehensible – and both Moore Street and adjoining Henry Street have their complement of slightly less legitimate hawkers peddling toys, curios, perfumes, jewellery or watches. Famous-name brands at bargain prices may be in evidence, but their authenticity is very dubious. Henry Street, next to the General Post Office, is a pedestrian mall with branches of most leading European chainstores.

UPPER O'CONNELL STREET

This northern section of O'Connell Street is graced by the **Anna Livia Millennium Fountain** situated in its central mall. Commissioned in 1988 for the city's millennium, it shows the spirit of the Liffey as a female figure rising from the waters. Local wits have dubbed it 'the Floozie in the Jacuzzi'. To the north of it is a statue of a more serious-looking clerical gentleman, Father Theobald Matthew (1790–1856), the noted Irish temperance cam-paigner. Judging by the number of pubs in Dublin, his preaching seems to have made little impact. A third statue, at the junction of O'Connell Street and Parnell Street, is of Charles Stewart Parnell (1846–91), leader of the 19th-century campaign for Home Rule.

FESTIVALS AND EVENTS
March 17 ●
St Patrick's Day.
Holiday, parades, live music
March ●
Dublin Film Festival
April ●
Irish Opera Spring Season
Irish Grand National
June 16 ●
Bloomsday celebrates works
of James Joyce
June ●
International Organ Festival
Budweiser Irish Derby
July ●
Dublin Regatta, Liffey
Powerboat Race
August ●
Dublin Horse Show
September ●
Dublin Theatre Festival

Below: *Moore Street's colourful produce market.* **Opposite:** *The 19th-century General Post Office, where the Easter Rising started.*

Right: *O'Connell Street is north Dublin's main artery.*
Opposite: *The Rotunda Hospital is a Parnell Square landmark.*

St Mary's Pro-Cathedral ★

Built just before Catholic emancipation in 1829, this is Dublin's largest Catholic place of worship, but is of interest more for its historic importance than for the elegance of its design. It was originally designed for O'Connell Street but contemporary religious prejudice relegated it to a side street.

PARNELL SQUARE AND AROUND

The south side of Parnell Square, next to the junction of Parnell Street and O'Connell Street, is taken up by the 18th-century Rotunda Hospital. Built between 1751 and 1755, it was the first purpose-built maternity hospital in Europe. On the north side of the square is the **Garden of Remembrance**, a memorial to the dead of Ireland's long struggle for independence. The centrepiece is a mighty sculpture by Oisin Kelly, representing the Children of Lir, characters out of Irish mythology. At the northeast corner of the Square is the Abbey Presbyterian Church. With its prominent neo-Gothic spire, it is a handy landmark.

Gate Theatre **

The Gate Theatre, in a Georgian building opposite the Rotunda, opened in 1930 and quickly established a reputation for staging adventurous and challenging plays. The Gate fostered the careers of a number of world-famous names – among them, Orson Welles and James Mason – and continues to be Dublin's most innovative theatre. Open for performances.

Dublin Writers Museum ***

This museum was opened in 1991 – Dublin's year as European City of Culture – to celebrate the city's writers through the ages. It is housed in a grand 18th-century townhouse, which is well worth a visit in its own right, and is stuffed with fascinating personal memorabilia, manuscripts, first editions and portraits of Irish writers and story-tellers from ancient times to the present.

Pride of place is given to displays and collections about the city's literary Nobel Prize winners, **George Bernard Shaw**, **W B Yeats** and **Samuel Beckett** (all of whom, ironically, spent more time away from Dublin than in it). A fourth display is being prepared on **Seamus Heaney**, who in 1995 became the latest Irish writer to win the Nobel Prize for Literature.

As well as temporary exhibitions and a gallery of portraits and busts, the museum has its own bookshop, restaurant and coffee shop, so is a good place for a coffee-break. The museum also has a year-round schedule of talks, readings, concerts and workshops. Open year-round Monday–Saturday 10:00–17:00, Sunday and holidays 11:30–18:00. Late opening until 19:00 Monday–Friday, June–August.

OSCAR WILDE

Oscar O'Flahertie Wills Wilde (1854–1900) was educated at Trinity College but began to gain notoriety as an aesthete and a daring dramatist at Magdalen College Oxford. His best known works of fiction include *The Picture of Dorian Gray* (1891), and plays including *Lady Windermere's Fan* (1892), *A Woman of no Importance* (1893) and *The Importance of Being Earnest* (1895) all of which in different ways poked fun at the British class system. A scandal surrounding his homosexuality led to his imprisonment, 1895–97, and he spent the rest of his life in exile in France.

BLOOMSDAY

If you are visiting Dublin in June, you can take part in the various Bloomsday events that are staged in the city. James Joyce first took out his future wife, Nora Barnacle, on 16 June 1904. Later, in his novel *Ulysses*, he chronicled the events that befall the Dubliner Leopold Bloom during this single day. Dublin celebrates 'Bloomsday', as it is known, each year on 16 June with readings, including performances of Molly Bloom's controversial soliloquy, to guided walks charting Bloom's progress around the city and taking in several Joyce sites.

Opposite: *James Joyce's great grandniece, Jessica Reynolds, held by her mother in front of the James Joyce Centre on Bloomsday.* **Below:** *The* Auld Dubliner, *one of Dublin's more than 700 atmospheric bars.*

National Wax Museum

This slightly eccentric museum features wax effigies of famous Irish and international figures – it is perhaps the only place you will see the Rev Dr Ian Paisley and His Holiness Pope John Paul II in the same room, or James Joyce, W B Yeats, George Bernard Shaw and Sean O'Casey around the same table – a grisly torture museum in the best waxwork tradition of grand guignol, and a collection of Irish sports memorabilia including autographed hurleys and football boots. The main section of the museum, however, contains wax figures of nationalist leaders including Robert Emmett, Wolfe Tone, Charles Stewart Parnell, the leaders of the Easter Rising, and the presidents and premiers of Ireland since independence. There is also, for some reason, a life-size copy in wax of Leonardo da Vinci's *'The Last Supper'*. Open Monday–Saturday 10:00–17:30.

Hugh Lane Municipal Gallery of Modern Art **

Named after its founder, this collection dates from 1908 and has been located at its present premises since 1930. The museum has a broad collection of modern works by Irish and European artists. There is a good collection of Impressionist works by Manet, Monet, Degas and others. The museum is housed in Charlemont House, which was designed for Lord Charlemont by Sir William Chambers in the mid 18th century, and was restored in 1991. Open Tuesday–Friday 09:30–18:00, Saturday 09:30–17:00, Sunday 11:00–17:00.

King's Inns **

The third of James Gandon's trio of important public buildings, and among the finest relics of Georgian Dublin, this splendid classical building houses Dublin's Inns of Court, the headquarters of the Irish legal profession. Its elegant dining hall and library are not normally open to the public, but its fine proportions may be admired from the surrounding gardens. Open Monday– Friday 09:00–18:00.

James Joyce Cultural Centre **

This 18th-century townhouse has been painstakingly restored as a shrine to the author of *Ulysses* and *Dubliners*. The centre aims to increase interest in Joyce's life and his sometimes impenetrable work – a welcome change from the not-so-distant past when *Ulysses* was banned in Ireland because it was considered obscene. Published in 1922, Joyce's hefty tome recounts, through the stream of consciousness style of writing which the author pioneered, the events of a single day – 16 June , 1904 – through the eyes of the book's central character, Leopold Bloom, and a handful of other protagonists. June 16 is cele–brated as '**Bloomsday**' in Dublin with readings from *Ulysses*, re-enactments of events in the book, and actors playing the parts of Joycean characters, wandering the streets in costume.

Mountjoy Square

This small square east of Parnell Square has the distinction of being Dublin's first Georgian square. It is named after Luke Gardiner, Viscount Mountjoy, who was one of the driving forces behind the planning of Georgian North Dublin. Until recently, Mountjoy Square was sadly derelict, but with a new awareness that the city's architectural heritage is worth preserving, many of its buildings are being restored, though many still appear close to collapsing.

DUBLIN BARS

Dublin bars (not usually called pubs by Dubliners) are absolutely essential to the city's character, humour and lifestyle and many of the finest have escaped the modernization of the city centre. The most atmospheric have retained many of their original features – carved mahogany bars, marble counters, heavy, elaborately decorated mirrors and frosted glass – and no visit to the city is complete without an evening in one of them. Dublin's commitment to pub life is evident in the huge number of bars in the city – more than 700 of them, or around one bar per thousand Dubliners.

ALONG THE QUAYS
Custom House **

Before setting off into the streets north of the river, pause to admire the painstakingly restored Custom House. It was completed in 1791 and designed by James Gandon, who was also responsible for two other fine buildings dating from the late 18th and early 19th centuries, the Four Courts and the King's Inns. The superbly proportioned Doric portico is flanked by carved stone busts, each representing one of Ireland's great rivers, and the building is crowned by a 38m (125ft) copper dome atop which stands a bronze statue representing Commerce. The Custom House took ten years to build and its construction was fiercely opposed by a clique of corrupt merchants. Their opposition was so vehement that for a while the architect had to go armed for fear of attack. Custom House Quay is not open to the public.

Above: *The statue atop the Custom House dome represents Commerce.*
Below: *The Abbey Theatre.*

Abbey Theatre **

The modern Abbey Theatre, built in 1966, is no beauty, but the Abbey and Peacock theatres of Ireland's National Theatre Society have played a central role in the revival and

encouragement of Irish drama and writing since its foundation in 1904. The Abbey has provided a stage for generations of Irish playwrights from J M Synge (1871–1909) to leading modern playwrights like Brian Friel. The Abbey complex has two theatres – the 638-seater Abbey Theatre upstairs and the 157-seater Peacock Theatre downstairs. Open for performances.

Above: *The Four Courts, overlooking the Liffey.*

The Four Courts **

Like the Custom House, this splendid 18th-century courthouse was designed by James Gandon, but was virtually destroyed during the Civil War, when it was occupied by anti-Free State rebels and besieged by Irish government troops for two months. Giving up hope of starving the rebel garrison into surrender, the government eventually shelled the building. Restoration was completed in 1932 and today the building is the seat of the Irish Supreme and High Courts. The entrance hall is open to visitors and is immediately below the soaring dome. Open Monday–Friday 09:00–17:00, entrance hall only.

W B YEATS

William Butler Yeats (1865–1939) was born in Dublin but established his name as a poet after emigrating to London. Drawn back to Ireland by his Fenian sympathies, he was prominent in the campaign to revive a distinctive Irish culture, establishing the Abbey Theatre as a national institution and, after the failure of the 1916 rising, eulogizing its heroes in verse. He was awarded the Nobel Prize for Literature in 1923 and following Irish independence became a Free State senator (1922–28). In 1932 he founded the Irish Academy of Letters.

Above: *The entrance to the haunting vaults at St Michan's Church.*
Opposite: *Sign at Irish Whiskey Corner.*

St Mary's Abbey *

Founded in the 12th century, St Mary's was destroyed following the Protestant Reformation and Henry VIII's dissolution of the monasteries throughout England and Ireland. The ruined Chapter House is all that is left of the abbey, which was once the most important foundation of the Cistercian order in Ireland. It was here in 1534 that 'Silken Thomas' Fitzgerald, son of the Earl of Kildare, began the revolt against English rule which was to result in his defeat and execution. The defeat of the powerful Fitzgeralds ended almost half a century in which the Anglo-Irish aristocracy were virtually independent of the English crown. Until their open revolt, Henry VIII was unwilling to become involved in a full-scale war against Kildare and his followers. Open June–September, Wednesday 10:00–17:00.

St Michan's Church **

The original St Michan's was built in 1095 by Dublin's Christianized Vikings, but the present-day church is much more recent. Its foundations date from 1685–86, but it was extensively rebuilt in 1821 and again after being damaged in the fighting around the Four Courts during the Civil War, so most of what you see today is comparatively recent. The church has two claims to fame. The first is its fine 17th-century organ, on which **Handel** is claimed to have composed parts of his *Messiah*; the second is its grisly collection of mummified cadavers, reputedly preserved by the peculiarly dry air of the church crypts. Open Monday–Friday 10:45–12:45, 14:00–16:45, Saturday 10:00–12:45. Open mornings only November–March.

Irish Whiskey Corner ★★★

The former Bow Street whiskey distillery closed in 1972, but became the headquarters of Ireland's biggest whiskey maker, Irish Distillers.

One of the former Jameson's Whiskey warehouses has been converted into a fascinating exhibition centre with a model distillery and antique copper pot stills and equipment, bottles and labels. A 15-minute audiovisual presentation tells the story of how *uisce beatha* is made, and admission includes a glass of whiskey in the adjoining Ball of Malt Bar, which is decorated with fine, old, frosted and gilt advertising mirrors collected from some of Dublin's vanished Victorian bars. You can also go on to learn to be a qualified whiskey taster, with a certificate to prove it, which will give you the required self-confidence needed to practice your newly learned skills by extensive product testing in Dublin's hundreds of bars. Guided tours, May–October, Monday–Friday 11:00, 14:30, 15:30, Saturday 15:30.

IRISH COFFEE

A relatively recent addition to the repertoire of Irish food and drink – it was invented in the early 20th century – Irish coffee is a delicious, warming after-dinner drink. It is simplicity itself to make: put a generous tablespoon of sugar into a warmed, stemmed whiskey glass and pour in enough strong hot black coffee to dissolve it. Stir thoroughly, and add a good strong measure of Irish whiskey. To finish, slowly pour one tablespoon of cold double cream into the glass over the back of a spoon so it floats on top of the whiskey-flavoured coffee.

5
Phoenix Park and Kilmainham

While most of Dublin's historic sights are in the city centre, there is plenty to explore in the western city and like everywhere else in Dublin there are place names evocatively steeped in the broad sweep of Ireland and its long struggle for freedom.

Phoenix Park, the city's largest area of public greenery, is claimed to be the largest city park in Europe, offering a respite at any time of the year from the bustling streets of central Dublin. It is a favourite with the city's joggers and other sports players and watchers, with facilities for Gaelic football and hurling, polo, cricket, cycling and athletics.

The park is also the location of the residence of the President of Ireland and of the US ambassador. In 1882 it was notorious for the 'Phoenix Park Murders', when a nationalist group known as the 'Invincibles' assassinated Lord Frederick Cavendish, the British chief secretary for Ireland, and his deputy Thomas Burke. The assassins were captured, imprisoned and subsequently executed in nearby Kilmainham Gaol. Kilmainham is now predominantly a residential suburb on the south bank of the River Liffey, but generations of Irish patriots languished in its grim prison.

On a more cheerful note, the Guinness Museum and Hop Store is a repository of knowledge built around the potent brew which, for many, epitomises the spirit of Ireland and its people.

The River Liffey and the main road which runs parallel to it form the southern boundary of Phoenix Park and separate it from Kilmainham, south of the river. The Liffey

DON'T MISS

*** Irish Museum of Modern Art/The Royal Hospital Kilmainham:
Fine collection housed in a 17th-century building.
*** Kilmainham Gaol:
Ghostly shrine to the most tragic moments in Irish history.
*** Phoenix Park:
Vast expanse of woodland and lawns by the River Liffey.
** Dublin Zoo: One of the world's oldest zoos with many rare birds and animals.

Opposite: *Vast Phoenix Park, claimed to be the largest city park in Europe.*

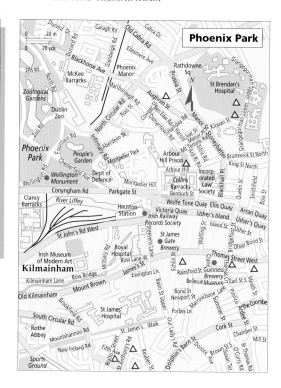

MURDER IN THE PARK

In 1882 a group calling themselves The Invincibles assassinated the newly-arrived British chief secretary, Lord Frederick Cavendish, and his under-secretary, Thomas Burke, in Phoenix Park, within sight of the viceroy's lodge (now the residence of the President). The murders were a severe setback to the cause of Irish Home Rule, threatening the fragile alliance between the British government of Gladstone and the Home Rule party led by Charles Stewart Parnell.

Below: *Tanks of the famous Irish Brew awaiting shipping to bars around the world.*

can be crossed by bridges at Victoria Quay, next to Heuston Station, and further from the centre at Islandbridge. South of the river, this part of the city is bordered in the east by the Liberties district, one of the oldest parts of Dublin.

KILMAINHAM AND AROUND
South of the River Liffey and Islandbridge Memorial Park lies Kilmainham. It is the site of two buildings which for very different reasons are virtually national shrines: Kilmainham Gaol and the Guinness Breweries.

Guinness Brewery, Hop Store and Museum ★★★

Founded in 1759 and frequently expanded and modernized since, the Guinness Brewery is a major feature of this part of the city and occupies a large site straddling James's Street. The museum, in nearby Crane Street, naturally celebrates Dublin's favourite brew – 10 million glasses produced daily around the world – but there is much more to its exhibitions than the making of Guinness.

Housed in a handsome four-storey 19th-century building, once utilized to store the hops used in flavouring Guinness, are the World of Guinness Exhibition, an audiovisual show on the history of Ireland's favourite beer, a transport museum and a bar in which to acquire this most Irish of tastes.

Two floors of the building are used for a lively year-round programme of art exhibitions. Guinness has been made here since 1759, when Arthur Guinness bought the Rainfords Brewery on this site and began production of the strong black brew with the creamy head. Open Monday–Saturday 10:00–17:30 and Sunday 14:30–17:30.

Above: *Memorabilia at the Hop Store and Museum.*
Below: *The famous Guinness Brewery.*

Irish Railway Records Society *

The excellent library of press cuttings and photographs is fascinating if you are interested in steam trains. The station, one of Dublin's two main rail termini, is a classic example of 19th-century railway architecture, completed in 1846. Open Tuesdays, 20:00–22:00.

Above: *The stylish courtyard of the Royal Hospital.*

Irish Museum of Modern Art/The Royal Hospital Kilmainham **

This fine collection is housed in an equally fine building. The Royal Hospital Kilmainham, built in 1684 as a hospice for military veterans, was still in use up until 1927. Architecturally similar to Les Invalides in Paris, with a wide expanse of inner courtyard and a stylishly-proportioned formal façade, the building was restored in 1986 and opened as the Museum of Modern Art in 1991. Its collection centres on the work of international and Irish 20th-century artists, with a strong programme of changing exhibitions. The Royal Hospital is the oldest secular, non-military, pre-18th-century building still standing in Ireland, and is the oldest intact classical building in the country. Features worth looking at include its grand banqueting hall and wood-panelled Baroque chapel. Open Tuesday–Saturday 10:00–17:30, Sunday 12:00–17:30.

Kilmainham Gaol ***

A fortress-like towered gateway is the landmark for this grim prison and shrine to the heroes of the Irish struggle for independence, located to the rear of the Royal Hospital, close to the River Liffey.

Once the main prison in British-occupied Ireland, it is now preserved as a memorial to men like **Robert Emmett, Charles Stewart Parnell, Eamon de Valera**

KILMAINHAM WALK

Start at Heuston Station, turning right as you leave the station, and turn left, following the signs to the Royal Hospital and the Irish Museum of Modern Art, which you enter by the front gate on St Johns Road. After visiting the hospital, leave by the rear gate and walk on to Kilmainham Gaol, then walk south to the entrance to the Islandbridge Memorial Garden. After visiting the garden, turn right along the River Liffey and cross the river to enter Phoenix Park, which offers a half-day's walking, including a visit to the Dublin Zoo.

and **James Connolly**, all of whom were incarcerated here. Some of them, like Parnell and de Valera, were lucky enough to walk out again. Others, like the leaders of the Easter Rising, were executed in Kilmainham's prison yard. From 1795 until 1924, Kilmainham was a potent symbol of British rule and Irish oppression. It is still a ghostly place to visit, and a reminder of the most tragic moments in Irish history, including the failed rebellions of 1798, 1803, 1848, 1867 and 1916.

The visit to the gaol includes an informative guided tour, an emotive audiovisual presentation and exhibition. Open May–September, daily 10:00–18:00, October–April, Monday–Friday and Sunday, 13:00–18:00.

THE FAIR CITY

The newest profile of Dublin is Peter Somerville-Large's *Dublin: The Fair City* (Cappaghlass, £25). Drawing freely on the writings of many literati, travellers and scholars associated with the city, Dublin-born Somerville-Large traces its history from the Vikings to the present day. It's a lively and erudite account, and with its hand-some photographs of Dublin's finest buildings it makes an excellent souvenir of your visit.

Drimnagh Castle

Originally built in the 13th century to house an Anglo-Norman garrison, this miniature stronghold, unusually, still has a water-filled moat – the only one in Dublin. It has been restored by *An Taisce* (National Trust for Ireland) and its medieval Great Hall with lofty ceiling and flagged floor, and its 17th-century gardens and surrounding buildings are open for viewing. Open April–October, Wednesday, Saturday, Sunday 12:00–17:00.

Below: *The grim interior of Kilmainham Gaol.*

WELLINGTON MONUMENT

Towering over Phoenix Park, the 64m (205ft) monument to Arthur Wellesley (1769–1852), first Duke of Wellington, is an ironic reminder of British rule. Though born in Dublin, Wellington never called himself Irish ("If I had been born in a stable, would that make me a horse?" he once asked). A very large proportion of Wellington's army in his successful campaigns in Spain and Portugal came from Ireland.

Below: *The Wellington Memorial in Phoenix Park.*

Islandbridge Memorial Park *

Across the river from Phoenix Park, on the River Liffey's South Bank, these beautifully laid out and recently-restored gardens commemorate the 49,400 Irishmen who died in the **1914–18 war** for the cause of the British Empire. The gardens were designed in 1931 by the English architect and landscape designer Sir Edward Lutyens. Open daily during daylight hours.

PHOENIX PARK ***

Phoenix Park, a vast expanse of woodland and lawns north of the River Liffey and 3km (2 miles) west of the city centre, is the largest city park in Europe, covering 709ha (1752 acres). The Duke of Ormond first established the park in 1662 as a deer park, and a herd of some 300 fallow deer is still resident. Deer are usually spotted in the wooded parts of the park. In 1745 Lord Chesterfield, then the owner, commissioned landscape architects to redesign the park's vistas in the then-popular Romantic manner, and in the 19th century the renowned landscape designer Decimus Burton added several contemporary touches.

Landmarks in the park include the 60m (195ft) obelisk of the Wellington Memorial, erected in 1817 to mark the triumphs of the Dublin-born Duke of Wellington in the Revolutionary and Napoleonic Wars. It stands close to the Parkgate entrance. In the midst of the park, another landmark is the towering Papal Cross, marking the spot where Pope John Paul II celebrated mass before a congregation of almost a million on his papal visit to Ireland in 1979. Visitor centre open November–mid March, Saturdays and Sundays only, 09:30–16:30, the rest of the year open daily between 09:30 and 17:00/17:30, last admission 45 minutes before closing.

Dublin Zoo *

In the heart of Phoenix Park, Dublin Zoo shelters a number of rare and endangered animal and bird species. One of the oldest zoos in the world, Dublin Zoological Gardens opened in 1830 and comprises 30 acres of landscaped grounds. High points of the zoo include a new reptile house, housing a collection of crocodiles, snakes, lizards, and amphibians and insects. There is a petting zoo where children can meet docile farmyard animals, and a miniature train circuit around the main sections of the zoo. Dublin Zoo takes part in a number of rare animal breeding programmes, and has a long track record in lion breeding – the snarling lion of the MGM movie logo was, the zoo claims, born here. Open weekdays 09:30–18:00, Sunday 10:30–18:00.

Ashtown Castle and Visitor Centre **

This restored 17th-century castle is the oldest building in the park. It now houses a visitor centre with informative displays on the history of Phoenix Park and future plans for its conservation and development. Open March, October, November, 09:30–17:00, April–May 09:30–17:30, June–September 09:30–18:30, December–February 09:30–16:30.

> **FLYING HIGH**
>
> Dublin's tourism boom has been fuelled by the huge increase in the number of airlines flying into the capital's airport. From the UK alone there are direct air services from 23 airports, including all five London airports, and because of fierce competition between airlines, fares are startlingly low. US visitors can save time on the way home by pre-clearing US Immigration formalities at Dublin Airport before departure, and with connections to 26 European destinations it has never been easier to make Dublin part of your tour of Europe.

Below: *Phoenix Park, a haven of greenery amid the bustle of central Dublin.*

6
Northside Suburbs and North Dublin Coast

Like the Grand Canal in southern Dublin, the **Royal Canal** flowing into the River Liffey forms a convenient boundary between central Dublin and its northern suburbs, while the River Tolka, joining the Irish Sea just north of the mouth of the Liffey, runs through the middle of the suburbs of Drumcondra and Marino.

The Northside suburbs contain Dublin's working-class heartland, where many city-centre slum-dwellers have been rehoused in the rebuilding of the city since the 1950s. This is the Dublin of Roddy Doyle's hilarious and touching novels and of some of western Europe's worst urban poverty. Unemployment is extremely high, particularly among young people, and the problems of the city's poorer districts are compounded by one of the highest rates of drug addiction in Europe. In contrast, the north Dublin seaside suburb of Howth, standing on a peninsula at the north point of Dublin Bay, is Dublin's most conspicuously wealthy neighbourhood.

Between the Royal Canal and the River Tolka lie a handful of sights worth seeing, while a wealth of natural and historic attractions are to be found dotted along the north coast between Howth and Drogheda, 48km (30 miles) north of Dublin.

GLASNEVIN

Straddling the River Tolka, Glasnevin is primarily a residential suburb, worth visiting for Dublin's outstanding botanic gardens, which rival the world-famous Kew Gardens in London.

DON'T MISS

*** National Botanic Gardens: Lovely gardens ablaze with colour year-round.
*** Casino Marino: Delightfully-restored 18th-century Palladian building.
*** Clontarf Castle: 12th-century tower and 19th-century castle on the site of a famous battle.
** North Bull Island: This island bird sanctuary shelters several rare and endangered species.

Opposite: *One of Ireland's most important fishing harbours, Howth.*

Northern Dublin

National Botanic Gardens ***

The fine gardens on the south bank of the River Tolka cover 20ha (47 acres). Rhododendrons, azaleas, roses and other flowering shrubs and bushes ensure a blaze of vivid colour for much of the year while in winter an array of impressive glasshouses provide shelter for tropical plants and for visitors.

The most impressive of these giant Victorian edifices is the **Great Palm House**, built in 1884 and recently restored to its former grandeur. The gardens contain more than 20,000 plant species from all over the world, ranging from rare orchids and tree-ferns to a 30m (100ft) Californian sequoia (the largest organisms on earth). Open summer, Monday–Saturday, 09:00– 18:00, Sunday 11:00–17:00, winter, Monday–Saturday 10:00–16:30, Sunday 11:00–16:30.

Prospect Cemetery (Glasnevin Cemetery) *

Across the road from the south entrance to the National Botanic Gardens, a round tower commemorates **Daniel O'Connell**, the great agitator and orator who founded the cemetery. Among the other illustrious Irish dead buried here are Charles Stewart Parnell, republican leaders Arthur Griffith and Michael Collins, Sir Roger Casement and Eamon de Valera. Open daily 08:30–17:30.

URBAN PROBLEMS

Ireland's economy in the 1990s shows signs of improvement, but unemployment is the country's biggest problem. Reaching 70% in Dublin's most deprived neighbourhoods, unemployment creates ghettoes on the fringes of the city and costs the Irish economy a fortune each year in social welfare programmes. Life in Dublin's unemployment-stricken communities was highlighted – perhaps even glamourized – in Alan Parker's film of Roddy Doyle's *The Commitments*, in which a group of young people on the dole form a rock band and almost make it.

MARINO

Just north of the mouth of the Tolka, the residential suburb of Marino has been built where several of Dublin's Anglo-Irish aristocratic families had their estates.

Casino Marino ★★★

Designed by the noted architect Sir William Chambers and built for Lord Charlemont, an Anglo-Irish noble-man, between 1767 and 1771, this delightful Palladian building has been restored, redecorated and furnished in period style. During the 18th century, the casino was used in its original Italian sense (little house) to denote an aristocrat's country retreat, and had not come to mean, as it does today, a gaming establishment. Cunningly designed, the building is much larger within than it appears from the outside; the proportions of the façade disguise two storeys and a basement, and the chimney-pots are concealed within decorative roof urns. Open June–September, daily 09:30–18:00.

Above left: *The gigantic Great Palm House at the National Botanic Gardens.*
Above right: *The cunningly designed Casino Marino.*

CLONTARF

Now a residential seaside suburb, Clontarf was the site of Brian Boru's victory over an alliance of his Irish and Norse rivals in 1014. The exact location of the battlefield is, however, unknown.

Clontarf Castle **

The tower of the first Clontarf Castle, built in the 12th century and occupied first by the Knights Templar and then by the Knights of St John, stands next to the much later castle, built in 1835. A grand baronial home, its gloomy mahogany interior is still intact and it is now a reception and banqueting centre. Open for private functions.

St Anne's Park *

At its most attractive in summer, when the rose gardens are in full bloom, St Anne's Park was laid out in the 19th century for Lord Ardilaun, a member of the Guinness brewing dynasty, and later bequeathed to the city. Landscaped woods surround an artificial lake.

North Bull Wall and Island **

A 900m (2950ft) breakwater constructed during the early 19th century to protect the Liffey Channel from silting, North Bull Wall brought into being a new island of sand dunes and salt marshes which built up on its north side. Part of North Bull Island is now a bird sanctuary and has been declared a UNESCO Biosphere Reserve. Up to 40,000 seabirds, waders and waterfowl – including rare Brent geese – shelter and nest here, their numbers boosted in winter by tens of thousands of migrants from beyond the Arctic Circle. The island's unique wetlands also foster growths of rare plant species including sea lavender, sea aster and glasswort. Open 24 hours daily. Visitor centre open daily 10:15–16:30.

Below: *A view of North Bull Wall, the breakwater which was built in 1820.*

HOWTH

Built on and around Howth Head, a craggy, 170m (530ft) headland jutting into the Irish Sea and protecting Dublin Bay from northerly gales, Howth started life as a fishing harbour in medieval times but has now become Dublin's wealthiest and most fashionable neighbourhood, with up-market restaurants and bars in the streets climbing up from its harbour, which remains one of Ireland's most important fishing ports.

Ship chandlers and fishing equipment suppliers along the harbourside indicate that this is still a working port, while a brand new marina and yacht club are signs of Howth's new upwardly-mobile population. There are fine views in all directions from the top of Howth Head, dramatic clifftop walks, and a number of historic sights.

The site has been settled since the neolithic (New Stone Age) era and its name comes from the Norse '*hoved*' meaning a headland. A 19th-century Martello Tower, built to protect against French invasion during the Napoleonic Wars, stands guard over the harbour, which is also overlooked by the tumbledown remains of St Mary's Abbey, dating from 1253.

Above: *Boats rest in attractive Howth harbour.*

ERSKINE CHILDERS

Erskine Childers (1870–1922), Irish author and yachtsman, supported the nationalist cause and used his yacht, the Asgard, to smuggle a cargo of 900 Mauser rifles into Howth from Germany to the Irish Volunteers in 1914. Despite his Republican loyalties, he served in the Royal Navy during World War I, going on to become a member of the first independent Dail. In 1922, with the outbreak of the Civil War, he followed Eamon de Valera into the anti-Free State IRA, and was captured and executed by the Free State government forces.

Above: *Howth Castle. The gardens are open to the public and are ablaze with brightly coloured rhododendrons in spring.*
Opposite: *The charming seaside resort of Malahide.*

Howth Castle Gardens **

The original Howth Castle dates from 1464, but its turreted walls are mostly 16th- and 18th-century additions. Only the grounds, with their brilliantly coloured rhododendron gardens, are open to the public. Open daily 08:00–sunset year round.

Visit the gardens in May to early June to see the glowing array of 2000 varieties of rhododendron in all their scarlet, crimson, pink, white and purple splendour. The gardens also contain a ruined square tower, Corr Castle, built in the 18th century, and a neolithic barrow locally known as Aideen's Grave.

National Transport Museum *

The museum is a treasure-trove for lovers of antiquated means of transport. Displays range from the elderly tram which once operated the Number 9 Hill of Howth service to one of the city's earliest fire engines, dating from 1889, and an assortment of other passenger and commercial vehicles from the 1920s and 30s. Open weekends and public holidays only, year round, 14:00–17:00.

MALAHIDE

Malahide, like other small towns north and south of Dublin, is gradually being transformed from a summer seaside resort into a residential neighbourhood. A large marina on the Broad Meadow estuary attracts yacht sailors, and the town has several good seafood restaurants.

Malahide Castle ***

Home of the Talbot family from 1185 until the death of the last Lord Talbot in 1973, the castle contains a collection

---

SAILING

Dublin Bay is ideal for yacht and dinghy sailing, with marinas at Malahide and Howth, where vintage Howth 17 class yachts are raced. The huge Dun Laoghaire harbour is an ideal place to learn the elements of sailing, and the base of the Irish National Sailing School, a year-round teaching and training centre specializing in sailing, windsurfing, powerboating and environmental studies.

of fine furniture – most of it from the 18th century – displayed in two elegant drawing rooms. There are also 17th- and 19th-century pieces, and an interesting assortment of portraits on loan from the National Gallery in Dublin. The castle is also said to be haunted by the ghost of one of the medieval family servants, known as Puck.

In the 300ha (741 acre) grounds, the 15th-century Church of St Sylvester is the last resting place of generations of Talbots, whose family vault contains a carved pre-Christian *sheela-na-gig*, a phallic stone fertility symbol. Open Monday–Friday 10:00–17:00, weekends and public holidays 14:00–17:00.

Fry Model Railway ***

Dublin in miniature, and a must for model train enthusiasts, the Fry Model Railway, housed in a special museum in the Malahide Castle grounds, has 4$^1/_2$km (2.8 miles) of track, making it one of the world's largest. It was begun by railway engineer Cyril Fry in the 1920s and is still growing, with a layout which covers 240m^2 (2500 sq ft). Models include not only detailed locomotives and rolling stock, but buses, ships, river barges, stations and bridges. Open year-round Monday–Friday 10:00–17:00, Saturday 11:00–18:00, Sunday and public holidays 14:00–18:00.

Malahide Botanic Garden **

The scenic 8ha (20 acre) gardens contain more than 5000 kinds of plant, most of them decorative, which are at their brightest in early summer. Open May–September, Monday–Friday 10:00–17:00, weekends and public holidays 14:00–17:00.

> **URBAN COWBOYS**
>
> You can buy a pony for just £100 in Dublin's Smithfield Market, and many people do – there are more than 2000 horses and ponies in the housing estates on the outskirts of the city. It is not unusual to see groups of young bareback riders clattering down the suburban streets of Tallaght or Ballyfermot, or to see ponies grazing on patches of greenery among the tower blocks or in small front gardens. The Dublin Society for Prevention of Cruelty to Animals claims many are mistreated, and wants tighter controls, but for most of the youngsters who own them, the horses are the only recreation and entertainment available – an alternative to drugs and petty crime.

SWORDS

A short distance inland from Malahide, Swords is one of
the oldest Christian settlements in Ireland, founded in
512 by St Colmcille, one of St Patrick's successors in the
mission to convert the Irish. Today, it is a pretty village
with some attractive 19th-century architecture.

Swords Castle and Round Tower *

More a fortified palace than a castle, this was one of the
seats of the Archbishops of Dublin, who had vast estates
in the area. Begun in the early 13th century, it was
expanded several times in following centuries, but only
the crumbling exterior walls survive. The adjacent 23m
(75ft) Round Tower dates from the early Christian era.

DONABATE

Donabate is a tiny village set on a magnificent peninsula
with, on its east side, one of the finest beaches to be
found north of Dublin.

Newbridge House and Demesne ***

Located 0.8km (¹/₂ mile) north of Swords, Newbridge
House, set in 156ha (385 acres) of landscaped parkland, is
one of the finest surviving 18th-century buildings in
Ireland. The Georgian drawing room, with its fine proportions, stucco and woodwork and elegant furnishings,
is a reminder of the style in which the Anglo-Irish aristocracy lived in their heyday, while the kitchen and laundry
on the lower floor show
where the work of keeping
them in luxury went on.

Off a square, cobbled
courtyard, a coach house
contains an ornate stage
coach dating from 1790 and
an 18th-century charabanc
built for the Duke of
Manchester. Around the
courtyard too are a carpen-
ter's shop, a forge, dairy and

estate workers house, and next to the mansion is an 8ha (20 acre) working farm stocked with native Irish farmyard breeds. Audiotape tours guide visitors through the rooms and grounds of the house. Open April–September Tuesday–Friday 10:00–17:00, Saturday 11:00–18:00, Sunday and public holidays 14:00–18:00.

LUSK

Lusk is a small farming town, with a medieval church and heritage centre highlighting its history, which stretches back to the earliest Christian times, when the missionary St MacCullin founded a monastery here.

Lusk Round Tower and Heritage Centre **

Lusk's small 19th-century church has an unusual, square, 16th-century belfry with four round towers of which one dates from the 6th century, making it one of Ireland's earliest surviving buildings. The belfry houses the Lusk Heritage Centre, with an interesting exhibition on the area's many medieval churches. Open mid-June–September, daily 10:00–18:00.

SKERRIES

A pretty fishing port and a large seaside resort, Skerries hums with visitors from Dublin and elsewhere in Ireland in summer, drawn by a long, sandy beach with shallow water. Three small offshore islands – Shenick's Island, Colt Island and St Patrick's Island, with a ruined church reputedly built by the saint himself – make for a charming view from the shore.

Midway between Skerries and the nearby village of Balbriggan, Ardgillan Castle is a grand, turreted 18th century country manor in equally magnificent landscaped grounds looking out over the Bay of Drogheda. Recently restored and furnished in Victorian style with a military history theme – uniforms, weapons and other militaria and paintings of battle scenes adorn each room – the ground floor drawing-room, morning room,

Above: *The sumptuous interior of Ardgillan Castle.*
Opposite: *Set on beautifully landscaped grounds is the 18th-century Ardgillan Castle.*

SWORDS

St Columba founded a monastic settlement at Swords, with a flourishing monastery so wealthy it was known as the 'Golden Prebend'. The round tower was built by the monks to protect their patrimony. When Brian Boru was killed at the battle of Clontarf in the 12th century, his body was brought to the monastery and kept there overnight.

THE DROGHEDA MASSACRE

In 1649, Drogheda became
the scene of Oliver
Cromwell's most violent
and bloody Irish slaughter.
After crushing the staunch
resistance, he went on to
massacre over 3000 of the
town's inhabitants including
women and children. On
discovering that almost 100
of the townsfolk had taken
refuge in the steeple of St
Peter's Church, Cromwell
burnt the entire building,
saying, 'a righteous judg-
ment of God upon these
barbarous wretches'.

dining room and library are open to visitors. In the
grounds are an attractive rose garden and herb garden,
and there are guided tours of the gardens in summer.
Do not miss the fine views southeast across the bay and
north to the Mountains of Mourne. Open April–
September, Tuesday–Sunday and public holidays 11:00–
18:00, October–March, Wednesday–Sunday and public
holidays 11:00–16:30; guided tours, mid-May–mid-
September, Saturday 15:30–16:30. Park open year-round
10:00–dusk.

DROGHEDA

Set on hills straddling the River Boyne estuary,
Drogheda is one of Ireland's oldest settlements, with
evidence of human habitation dating back at least two
millennia. Like Dublin, it has suffered from insensitive
development, with a new road system which has

annihilated much that was of historic interest, but its smaller back lanes and harbour area are worth wandering through. Oliver Cromwell's Parliamentary troops sacked the town in 1649, slaughtering more than 1000 men, women and children in revenge for the massacre of Irish Protestants during the so-called 'Queen's Rising' of 1641. In the later conflict (1689–90) between the deposed King James II and William of Orange (William III), Drogheda was fortunate enough to choose the winning side.

Opposite: *The town of Drogheda, straddling the River Boyne.*
Below: *St Laurence's Gate, the finest surviving portion of Drogheda's city walls.*

Millmount Museum **

Pride of place is given to the sword and mace presented to the burghers of Drogheda by King William III of England after the Battle of the Boyne in 1690. Other interesting exhibits include tools, weapons and regalia of the city's craft guilds, trade union banners, maps and documents. Climb the courthouse tower for a fine view of Drogheda, the river and the bay. Open summer, daily 10:00–13:00, 14:00–17:00, winter, Wednesday, Saturday, Sunday 15:00–17:00.

St Peter's Church

The church is not outstandingly attractive but is of historic interest for its shrine of St Oliver Plunkett, Archbishop of Dublin, executed after being falsely accused of treason during the anti-Catholic hysteria of 1681 and later canonized. A grisly relic, the saint's head in a bejeweled casket is venerated by Catholic pilgrims. St Peter's Church, West Street. Open daily 09:00–18:00.

7
South Dublin Suburbs and Dublin Bay Coast

The southern crescent of the tree-lined Grand Canal, built in the 18th century to connect the city with the Shannon, Ireland's most important river, forms a boundary around the inner city. Beyond the canal lie the suburbs of the city's green belt.

Dublin Bay sweeps in a 13km (8 mile) crescent from the mouth of the River Liffey to the Dalkey headland. Along its coast, several small towns – each with its own strong historic and literary associations – have merged in the past 30 years into a suburban seaside strip stretching south as far as Dun Laoghaire, the main port for ferries to England and Wales, and beyond to the beaches of Killiney Bay. Inland lies very fertile farming country and the rolling slopes of the beautiful Dublin Mountains.

BALLSBRIDGE

This mature South Dublin residential area takes its name from the old bridge over the River Dodder, which was reputedly close to the home of a certain Mr Ball. The bridge gave him a modest immortality, as nothing more is known about him.

Landsdowne Road Stadium

Ballsbridge is best known as the location of Landsdowne Road, Ireland's international rugby/football stadium. The park which surrounds the rugby ground is bisected by the Dublin Area Rapid Transit (DART) line. The stadium is also used for other events, but comes into its

DON'T MISS

*** National Maritime Museum: Fascinating maritime collection displayed in a fine, converted 19th-century church.
*** James Joyce Tower and Museum: Unique museum dedicated to Joyce's life and works.
*** Rathfarnham Castle: Built in 1585 as an archbishop's residence with an extravagant Rococo interior.
** Chester Beatty Collection: Magnificent collection of Oriental and Asiatic art.

Opposite: *Yachts moored at the Royal Irish Yacht Club at Dun Loaghaire.*

HORSE SHOW

The Dublin Horse Show, held in the first week of August, is a major event in a country where horse racing attracts a fanatical following. Irish-bred horses are sought-after worldwide, commanding high prices and earning the country £6 million a year in foreign currency. The biggest racing events on the calendar are the Irish Grand National, held at Fairhouse, west County Dublin. Dublin has two racecourses of its own, one in Phoenix Park, the other in the southwestern suburb of Leopardstown.

own each year during the Five Nations championship in which Ireland's rugby team – which is drawn not only from the republic but from the six counties of Northern Ireland too – pits its skills in an exciting, internationally televised contest against Scotland, England, Wales and France. Open for matches.

Herbert Park

A short distance south of Landsdowne Road is Herbert Park, the 13ha (32 acre) site of the 1907 Dublin International Exhibition, an early attempt to put the city firmly on the 20th-century commercial map. The small but pretty park surrounds a large boating pond, which was a central feature of the 1907 show and is its only relic. Colourful flower gardens make Herbert Park most attractive in spring and summer. The park is open to the public 08:00–closing time, which varies according to the season – winter closing time at 17:30, summer closing time at 22:00 and mid-season closing time at 19:00.

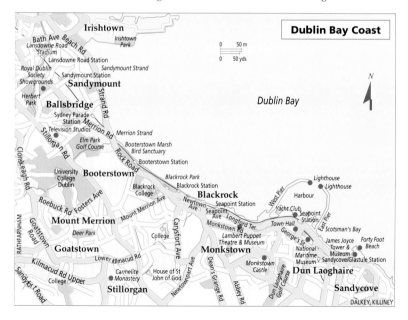

Royal Dublin Society (RDS) *

The ample grounds which surround this sturdy 19th-century stone building with its dignified classical façade and portico are used annually for the **Dublin Horse Show**, the best known internationally of an extensive calendar of events and indoor trade exhibitions. Founded in 1731, the society has played an important part in the life of the city, helping to found some of Ireland's most important scholarly and cultural institutions, including the National Museum, the National Library and the National College of Art.

Above: *The Dublin Horse Show is an internationally famous event. Horse racing, show-jumping, and horse sales attract an enormous following in Ireland.*

The RDS moved to Ballsbridge in 1922 from its former headquarters in Leinster House (*see* page 54), which became the seat of the first Free State government and is still the meeting place of the Dail.

Chester Beatty Library **

There is nothing Irish about the Chester Beatty collection, a magnificent ensemble of Oriental and Asiatic art which was given to the city by American-born millionaire, Sir Alfred Chester Beatty (1875–1968). Sir Alfred, a great lover of Ireland, travelled extensively in Asia and amassed an eclectic collection which ranges from priceless Persian manuscripts to hundreds of delicate Chinese snuff bottles.

The gallery is well worth the journey from the city centre, especially if you have any interest in Asian art and culture. If you do not, it may prove an even more inspiring eye-opener. On display are paintings, costumes, carvings, wall hangings and clay tablets, among other objects, and the collection spans eras from ancient Babylon (2700BC) to modern times. High points of the visit are the glowing Japanese prints, and the collection of Islamic art is said to be one of the finest in the world. Open Tuesday–Friday 10:00–17:00, Saturday 14:00–17:00, free guided tours Wednesday and Saturday 14:30.

Note: The library is due to move to Dublin Castle; phone (01) 269 2386 for further information.

COLLECTORS FAIRS

Serious souvenir hunters should time their visit to coincide with the regular Dublin and District Antiques and Collectables Fairs, where you can bargain for everything from toys, jewellery and silverware, prints and paintings, stamps and coins, furniture and antiquarian books to antique armour and weapons. Fairs are held several times a year in Dublin and Dun Laoghaire. For dates and times tel: (01) 496 4390.

BOOTERSTOWN

A quiet residential suburb close to the Irish Sea, Booterstown's main point of interest for the visitor is its wildfowl reserve.

Booterstown Marsh Bird Sanctuary

This small 4ha (2 acre) waterfowl sanctuary on the outskirts of the city is maintained by the Irish Wildbird Conservancy and the National Trust for Ireland. Keen birders can get closer to a variety of common and rare ducks, geese, grebes and wading birds by crossing the footbridge at Booterstown DART station to the sea wall, where the tidal sands of Dublin Bay attract vast flocks of birds, many of which nest and roost in the attractive reserve.

BLACKROCK

It comes as no surprise that this pleasant seaside suburb, a popular and elegant resort in Dublin's Georgian heyday, is named after the craggy Black Rock, just offshore. There is, unfortunately, little remaining of Blackrock's 18th-century elegance. Most of its older buildings – including Frescati, home of the nationalist hero Lord Edward Fitzgerald, who was executed for his part in the rising of 1798 – have been demolished to make way for dull modern residential suburbs and shopping complexes.

Blackrock Park, at the corner of Rock Road and Mount Merrion Avenue, has fine views of Dublin Bay. Just north of the town centre, **Blackrock College** is one of the oldest Catholic colleges in Ireland. Founded in 1860, its former pupils include IRA leader, later president, Eamon de Valera, and rock star Bob Geldof, among a host of other famous Irish names.

MONKSTOWN

Merging with Blackrock is Monkstown, another dormitory suburb overlooking Dublin Bay and with a string of bathing places lining its sweep of beach, along Seapoint Avenue.

BRIAN O'NOLAN

Brian O'Nolan (1911–66), better known by his pen names of **Flann O'Brien** and **Myles na gCopaleen**, was brought up in Blackrock and educated at Blackrock College and University College, Dublin. Both his novels and short stories, written as Flann O'Brien, and his column for the Irish Times, as Myles na gCopaleen, exhibit a weird and uniquely Irish surrealism in which fictional characters live in the author's home and steal his cigarettes, men gradually transmute into bicycles, and ventriloquists form a trade union to blackmail their patrons. Both *The Third Policeman* and *The Dalkey Archive* are set in the South Dublin suburbs.

Culturlann na hEireann (Irish Cultural Institute)

The institute is the centre of *Comhaltas Ceoltoiri Eireann*, the cultural movement which does most to revive and keep alive Irish folk culture. In summer, it can be one of the best places in Dublin to enjoy Irish fiddle music and you can also learn to dance traditional Irish jigs and reels. Open during summer (June–end August) for performances of traditional music, singing and dance.

Monkstown Castle *

Built in the 13th century to defend the lands of the Cistercian monastery which once stood near here, this is no grand castle but a functional miniature stronghold. The fortifications still standing include the keep (defensive tower), gatehouse and a section of wall. Open Monday–Saturday 09:00–17:00.

Lambert Puppet Theatre and Museum **

Eugene and Mai Lambert opened Ireland's first puppet theatre in their home, a Victorian mansion in Monkstown, in 1972 and expanded the auditorium to seat 300 in 1984. In 1994, they added a puppet theatre and teaching studio upstairs. The museum contains an amazing collection of marionettes from all over the world, from traditional Indonesian *wayang* puppets to modern inventions used in dozens of puppet plays for adults as well as children, including works by W B Yeats and Oscar Wilde. Open Monday–Saturday 09:30–17:00.

DUN LAOGHAIRE

Dun Laoghaire (pronounced Dun Leary) is claimed to have been the seat of a 5th-century Irish king named Laoghaire who was converted to Christianity by St Patrick. In the early 19th century it was renamed Kingstown, in honour of King George IV's visit to Ireland

> **BOOTERSTOWN MARSH**
>
> Booterstown Marsh is a refuge for huge numbers of seabirds and waders, including snipe, sanderling, dunlin and bar-tailed godwit. Black terns visit in autumn and roseate terns are often seen. There is also a large gull population which can include Mediterranean gulls and occasionally ring-billed gulls, windblown visitors from the US.

Below: *A cannon stands poised at Dun Laoghaire's mid-19th-century harbour.*

Opposite: *The charming bay at Sandycove with the James Joyce Tower.*

in 1821. Just over a century later, with the coming of independence, it reverted to its old Irish name. Its enormous harbour, built in the mid-19th century, is more than a mile across and is ample for the Irish Sea ferry fleet which operates from here to British ports and for the flotilla of yachts moored offshore from the clubhouse of the Royal Irish Yacht Club.

Just south of the harbour, **Scotsman Bay** commemorates John Rennie, the Scottish harbour engineer who designed the grand harbour and oversaw its construction, which was completed in 1859.

Dun Laoghaire's most impressive thoroughfare is Marine Road, where three elegant 19th-century buildings – the Post Office, the Town Hall with its graceful clock tower, and St Michael's Church – are worth a glance in passing.

JAMES JOYCE

James Augustine Aloysius Joyce (1882–1941) was born and educated in Dublin, where several of his novels and stories are set, but spent most of his life abroad, leaving for Paris in 1902 and returning only briefly between 1903–4. His early books *Chamber Music* (1907) and *Dubliners* (1914) won critical acclaim. The later *Ulysses* (1922) was attacked by literary and religious conservatives both for its revolutionary 'stream of consciousness' style and passages which, while tame-seeming today, were then regarded as shocking. *Finnegans Wake*, in which he developed the 'stream of consciousness' style of writing pioneered in *Ulysses*, was published in 1939. *Dubliners* is the easiest to read of Joyce's works, *Finnegans Wake* the most impenetrable, but all his work is marked by flashes of Dublin wit and literary lyricism.

National Maritime Museum ***

Guaranteed to fascinate anyone with even a slight interest in the sea, this museum has the added attraction of being housed in a lovely historic building, the former Mariners' Church, built in 1837. High points include the **Great Baily Light Optic**, the lens from the Baily Lighthouse on the Howth Peninsula, just north of Dublin. The **Halpin Collection**, donated to the Maritime Institute by the family of Captain Robert Halpin, the Irish master of the *Great Eastern*, includes a 3m (10ft) scale model of the historic 19th-century iron steamship designed by Isambard Kingdom Brunel.

A 10m (33ft) longboat, captured from the French frigate *Resolue* in 1796 during the French expedition to support the rising of the United Irishmen, is also on display, as is a model of the Sirius, the first ship to make a transatlantic crossing powered only by steam. Other relics include logbooks and equipment from U-19, the German submarine which landed the nationalist conspirator Sir Roger Casement – who was born at nearby Sandycove – on his ill-fated return to Ireland in 1916. Open May–September, Tuesday–Sunday 14:30–17:30, October–April, Saturday–Sunday 14:30–17:30.

SANDYCOVE

Sandycove, only 1km (900yd) south of Dun Laoghaire's massive East Pier, has a pretty little harbour – nowadays more used by yachts than by the fishing smacks for which it was built – and a small beach between rocky headlands which lives up to its name, though only by coincidence.

Forty Foot Beach *

Forty Foot beach is in fact a bit longer than that, and is said to have been named after the 40th Regiment of Foot (infantry) who were garrisoned nearby during the 19th century. For more than a century, the beach has been a men-only bathing spot, where gentlemen who are so inclined can swim nude in what James Joyce, who briefly lived nearby, described invitingly as the 'snotgreen, scrotum-tightening sea.' Dublin feminists have taken a few well-publicised dips there in recent years, shocking local sensibilities and titillating the Irish media.

> **CHILLY DIP**
>
> The hardiest Dubliners celebrate Christmas Day with an early morning swim at **Forty Foot**, the small beach below James Joyce's tower at Sandycove where skinny-dipping (formerly men only, now open to women too) has been a tradition for decades. Few stay in the chilly Irish Sea for more than a few minutes, and when honour is satisfied, a drop of Powers or Jameson's helps to fend off hypothermia.

Sir Roger Casement's Birthplace ★

At 29 Lawson Terrace, Sandycove Road, a blue plaque marks the birthplace of Sir Roger Casement, convicted of treason for seeking German aid for the nationalist movement and hanged in 1916.

James Joyce Tower and Museum ★★★

The squat round tower overlooking the sea at Sandycove is one of a series of Martello towers, small fortresses built at strategic landing-places around the coasts of Ireland and mainland Britain in 1804 to defend against the threat of a French invasion. Built to a standard plan, each tower is 13m (40ft) high with granite walls 2¹/₂m (8ft) thick and a single door 3m (10ft) above ground level.

Designed to enable a small garrison to hold off enemy landing parties until help arrived, the towers never had to prove themselves and most fell into disuse. A century after it was built, however, this particular one gained a place in literary history when James Joyce

---

SIR ROGER CASEMENT

Sir Roger Casement (1864–1916) was born in Sandycove. Though employed in the British colonial service, he was a convinced Irish patriot and humanitarian, denouncing the treatment of native workers both in Africa and in Brazil, where he was British Consul-General. He was knighted in 1911, but joined the nationalist Irish Volunteers in 1913. When World War I began he sought German help for the Easter Rising but on returning to Ireland in April 1916 he was captured, convicted of treason and hanged.

came to stay as a guest of the writer Oliver St John Gogarty, later making it the setting for the first chapter of his most famous novel, *Ulysses*.

Since 1962, the tower has been a museum dedicated to Joyce's life and works, and contains a treasury of fascinating Joycean memorabilia, including letters and manuscripts, the writer's waistcoat, tie and guitar, and – a macabre touch – Joyce's death mask. There is a unique library of rare first editions of almost all of Joyce's writing, including a first edition of the original 1922 edition of *Ulysses* and an edition with line illustrations by Henri Matisse. Open April–October, Monday–Saturday 10:00–13:00 and 14:00–17:00, Sunday 14:00–18:00.

DALKEY

The prettiest of the South Dublin coastal suburbs, Dalkey has plenty of individual character and – with two charming harbours – still feels like a real seaside village rather than an extension of urban Dublin.

In medieval times it was an important seaport, defended by extensive fortifications of which only the ruins of **Archibald's Castle** and its tower, on Castle Street, survive today. Also on Castle Street, next to Archibald's Castle, is the shell of the medieval **St Begnet's Church**, surrounded by a small graveyard full of eroded gravestones whose dates reach back to the Norman era.

Dalkey Island Bird Sanctuary **

About 1km (900yd) offshore from Coliemore Harbour, the granite walls of a round Martello tower, twin to the James Joyce Tower at Sandycove, rise from the highest point of Dalkey Island to command Dalkey Sound.

The tiny island is a bird sanctuary and the home of a herd of feral goats and there are several boat trips a day in summer from Coliemore Harbour. At the opposite end of the island from the Martello tower and the adjoining ruined barracks and gun emplacement stands the shell of the medieval St Begnet's Oratory, a ruined chapel and hermitage which was an annex of St Begnet's Church.

> **DALKEY'S HERITAGE**
>
> Dalkey was once known as the 'Town of Seven Castles', but only two of these now remain. The ruins of a number of others, however, can still be seen. Bulloch Castle overlooking Bullock Harbour was built by St Mary's Abbey in Dublin in the 12th century. Two more castles are on Castle Street – Goat Castle and Archibald's Castle. Over and above its historic castles, Dalkey has several holy wells, one of which – St Begnet's on Dalkey Island – is said to be able to cure rheumatism.

Opposite: *Colourful boats moored at Coliemore harbour, with Dalkey Island in the background.*

Shaw's Cottage *

Torca Cottage, Torca Road Dalkey Hill, is marked with a blue plaque noting that playwright George Bernard Shaw lived there as a boy between 1866 and 1874.

KILLINEY BAY AND KILLINEY HILL

Separated from Dalkey by the headland that marks the southern end of Dublin Bay, Killiney Bay is a beautiful sweep of sheltered beach. Overlooking it, Killiney Hill, between Dalkey and Killiney, is one of the Dublin area's most beautiful landscaped parks with a signposted nature trail and a scattering of decorative follies and monuments dating from the 18th and 19th centuries.

The highest point of the hill is marked by the **Mapas Obelisk**, built for Colonel John Mapas, who owned the estate which the park used to be, in 1742. Colonel Mapas commissioned the stone column to give work to local masons and labourers during the famine winter of 1741–42. On a clear day you may be able to see the Welsh mountains, almost 160km (100 miles) to the east from here. Close to it stands the **Wishing Stone**, a ziggurat built in 1852 which according to local legend will – under the right circumstances – grant your wish.

RATHFARNHAM

Some 8km (5 miles) inland from Killiney, Rathfarnham stands on the south bank of the River Dodder, on the very edge of the Dublin conurbation and is the starting point for one of the most worthwhile walks in Ireland, the Wicklow Way, which runs through the wild Dublin and Wicklow hill country for almost 130km (80 miles).

Rathfarnham Castle ***

Built in 1585 as an archbishop's residence, the castle was for many years used as a Jesuit college and has been extensively restored. The interior is extravagantly Rococo, with remarkable stucco friezes and ceilings and grandly spacious rooms. Next to it is Cromwell's Barn, a fortified 16th-century barn which the Parliamentary commander Oliver Cromwell is reputed to have used as headquarters during his notoriously vengeful campaign against the Royalist Irish in 1649. Open daily 10:00–18:00.

Pearse Museum *

St Enda's School (*Scoil Eanna*), housed in an 18th-century house, was founded in 1908 to promote Irish language and culture. Its founder and first headmaster, Padraic (or Patrick) Pearse (1879–1916) was prominent in the Irish Republican Brotherhood and commanded the rebel forces in the Easter Rising of 1916, for which he was tried and shot by the British, along with his brother William, who also fought in the Rising. The small museum commemorates Pearse's work as a teacher, author and poet. Open from November–January, daily 10:00–13:00 and 14:00–16:00; February–April, September–October, daily 10:00–13:00, 14:00–17:00; May–August, daily 10:00–13:00, 14:00–17:30.

HELL FIRE

Atop Montpellier Hill, near Killakee on the Rathfarnham/Glencree Road, stands the crumbling ruin of the Hell Fire Club, the meeting place of a group of dissolute 18th-century aristocrats. Drunkards, gamblers and womanisers to a man, they were also said to be devil-worshippers – a reputation they gleefully embraced. They are said to have set the building alight one night and carried on with their revelry within to live up to their name. Today, the hill is a popular picnic spot with fine views of the city and its coastline.

Opposite: *The strikingly beautiful sweep of Killiney Bay with its inviting, sheltered beach.*
Above: *The impressive, extensively restored Rathfarnham Castle.*

8
Around Dublin

County Dublin, a half-circle of territory surrounding the Irish capital, has something for everyone, from historic castles to brand-new championship golf courses, canalside strolls to challenging hill-walking country.

County Dublin (Co. Dublin) borders three other Irish counties – Co. Meath, to the north and northwest, Co. Kildare to the west and to the south Co. Wicklow. Dublin's river, the **Liffey**, rises in the Wicklow Mountains and takes the long way round to the city, curving in a loop through Co. Kildare before flowing into Dublin from the west. The **Royal Canal**, which flows through north Dublin, cuts County Dublin more or less in two and leads off westward, along the Meath-Kildare county line, while the **Grand Canal** leads off from the south Dublin suburbs through the Kildare countryside, eventually to meet Ireland's biggest river, the Shannon.

Six main highways radiate from Dublin, linking the capital with the rest of Ireland. Anti-clockwise, these are the N1 coastal highway north to Drogheda and the border with Northern Ireland; the N2 and N3, running northwest to Meath and beyond; the N4 and N7, leading respectively west and southwest through Kildare; and the N11 coast highway south through Wicklow.

Dotted around County Dublin are a score of villages and pretty market towns, each with its own attraction, whether a castle, great house, historic battlefield or scenic viewpoint. All are easy to get to from the city by rail, bus, or car, as no point in the county is more than 32km (20 miles), or about half an hour's drive, from central Dublin.

DON'T MISS

★★★ Glendalough Visitor Centre: Cradle of Irish Christianity, with 9th-century monastic buildings.
★★★ Newgrange Prehistoric Site: The most fascinating ancient archaeological site in Ireland.
★★★ Russborough House: Palatial 18th-century manor house in the Palladian style.
★★ Hill of Tara: Ancient standing stones mark the seat of Ireland's High Kings.

Opposite: *The splendid, landscaped gardens of Powerscourt Estate.*

Between Dublin and Wicklow, not far south of the city boundaries, lie the Dublin Mountains. Though mountains only in the Irish sense – no summit exceeds 1000m (3300ft) – this hilly, almost uninhabited country offers a welcome contrast to the bustling city life.

COUNTY DUBLIN
St Margaret's *

The residential suburb of St Margaret's, around Dublin Airport, claims to be golf capital of Ireland, with two fine 18-hole courses only 10km (6 miles) from Dublin city centre.

Open Golf Centre **

The 18-hole course was extended to 27 holes in 1995. The centre aims to make golf accessible to all, with facilities, course management techniques and professional tuition to compare with Ireland's best member clubs. Practice facilities include a 16-bay driving range. Open to visitors between 08:00 and sunset.

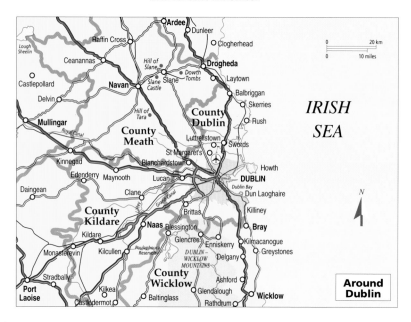

St Margaret's Golf and Country Club **

The beautiful 18-hole, par 73 course hosted the Women's Irish Holidays Open in 1994 and is regarded as one of the country's top-ranking courses, with challenging water hazards, undulating greens and contoured fairways. Open to visitors daily 08:00–sunset.

Hollystown Golf **

Just off the main N3 highway at Mulhuddart, 10km (6 miles) northwest of Dublin, this 18-hole, par 72 course is set into rich natural parkland well-endowed with mature trees, streams and ponds. Holes include three testing par 5s, a combination of par 4s and three varying par 3s, making the nominal par 72 an elusive target. Open to visitors daily 08:00–sunset.

Above: *St Margaret's Golf and Country Club.*

LUTTRELLSTOWN

Only 6km (4 miles) from central Dublin (and only 3km [1¹/₂ miles] from the Phoenix Park), this village suburb's main feature is its Anglo-Norman castle, which houses a fine hotel and golf course.

Luttrellstown Castle Golf and Country Club **

The 18-hole, par 72 course is set in the ancient parkland of Luttrellstown Castle is beautifully framed by the backdrop of the rolling Dublin Mountains. Planted with mature trees, the lovely estate also offers enchanting forest walks to golfers and non-golfers alike. The oldest part of the castle dates back to the 14th century, though its decorative turrets and battlements are from the 19th century. Open to visitors daily 08:00–sunset.

CYCLING

Cycling is a good way to explore the countryside in County Dublin and indeed throughout Ireland. The roads are relatively quiet, the environment unpolluted, and there is plenty of wildlife to look out for. Bicycles can be transported free on ferries to Ireland or you can hire one when you arrive. The leaflet, *Cycling Ireland*, available from Irish Tourist Board offices, gives details on bicycle hire and suggested cycle routes.

Below: *The Wicklow*
Way leads through lovely
mountain scenery.
Opposite bottom:
Rampant lions guard
Russborough House.

The Wicklow Way ★★★

One of the finest walks in Ireland, the Wicklow Way, leads in a north-south line from Marley Park, south of the city, along the eastern flanks of the Dublin Mountains and the rugged granite crags of the adjoining Wicklow Mountains to end some 130km (80 miles) later at Graiguemanagh in Co. Kilkenny. The clearly marked route leads through the largest area of untouched high country in Ireland and through tremendously varied scenery, from bare hillsides to narrow country lanes and woodland paths.

The going can be tough, as much of the route lies above the 500m (1500ft) level and follows old bog roads, forest firebreaks and cattle-drovers' trails. Proper walking boots, wet weather gear and a reliable map are essential. As always when walking in hilly country, make sure someone knows your next destination *en route* and when you expect to arrive there, and do not tackle the tougher, more remote stretches alone. Accommodation is available in youth hostels and country inns along the way (*see* Travel Tips/At a Glance).

THE WICKLOW WAY

One of the finest walks in Ireland, the Wicklow Way leads from Marley Park, south of the city, along the eastern flanks of the Dublin and Wicklow Mountains to end 130km (80 miles) south at Graiguemanagh in Co. Kilkenny. The route leads through the largest area of untouched high country in Ireland and through tremendously varied scenery. The going can be tough, as much of the route lies above the 500m (1500ft) level, following old bog roads and forest firebreaks. Essentials include good boots and wet weather gear. Accommodation is available in youth hostels and country inns along the way.

WICKLOW

Though only a short drive from Ireland's capital, County Wicklow is surprisingly empty of people. The Wicklow Mountains, with their bare hillsides and granite-bouldered glens, dominate the county – in glaring contrast to the busy streets of central Dublin, only half an hour's drive away.

Russborough House ***

Located near Blessington village (3km [2 miles] southwest of the village on N81 highway), the palatial Russborough mansion is the most splendid grand manor house in Ireland. Designed in the Palladian style popular in the first half of the 18th century, the magnificent rooms display fine stucco ceilings and the house is perfectly maintained and lavishly furnished with period pieces including bronzes, silverware and china, tapestries and antique furniture. Also on display is the fine **Beit Collection** of paintings, accumulated by the house's owner, South African millionaire Sir Alfred Beit. However, the finest works in the collection are on permanent loan to the National Gallery of Ireland in Dublin. Open Easter–May and October, Sunday and Bank Holidays, 10:30–17:30; June–September, daily 10:30–17:30.

Above: *Rural Dublin is only a short distance from the heart of the city.*

Above: *The Round Tower, Glendalough.*
Below: *There are waymarked walks around Glendalough.*

Glendalough Visitor Centre ★★★

This wooded valley in the Wicklow Mountains has a special place in the history of Christianity in Ireland, for it was here in AD545 that **St Kevin**, following in the footsteps of **St Patrick**, founded a monastery which survived until the English destruction of the monasteries in the 16th century. There is still plenty to see, and the sight is powerfully evocative of bygone centuries. A 33m (100ft) tall round tower with a conical roof provided the monks with a refuge when attacked by Viking or Irish raiders, and is Glendalough's most prominent landmark. Next to it stands the shell of the 9th-century cathedral and the 3.3m (10ft) St Kevin's Cross, dating from the mid-12th century and decorated with curling Celtic designs.

The Glendalough Visitor Centre has an exhibition and an interesting audiovisual show which help to put the site into its historic context. A guided tour of the site can also be arranged. In addition there are a number of waymarked walking routes among the glen's woods, lakes and waterfalls. Open mid-March–May, daily 09:30–18:00; June–August, daily 09:00–18:30; September–mid-October daily 09:30–18.00; mid-October–mid-March, daily 09:30– 17:00.

Avondale House ★★

Situated near Rathdrum, Co. Wicklow (1 mile from the village on R752 road), this attractive late-18th-century mansion with its blue-tiled roof, white stonework and elegantly-proportioned portico, was the family home of Charles Stewart Parnell, one of 19th-century Ireland's greatest men, whose advocacy of Irish self-rule made him a major political figure both in Ireland and in the British parliament.

Left: *Powerscourt Estate Gardens are among the region's finest sights.*

Now owned by the Irish Forestry Board, Avondale has been refurbished in mid-19th-century style and an audio-visual presentation shows the highlights of Parnell's life and demonstrates his importance to modern Ireland. Open daily May–September, 10:00–18:00, October–April 11:00–17:00.

Powerscourt Estate and Gardens ★★

Powerscourt House, the magnificent mansion on the estate, was destroyed by fire in the 1970s but its splendid landscaped gardens are among the region's finest sights, especially in spring and summer. The terraced gardens slope down in five tiers to the lakeside and are dotted with rare trees, most of them planted during the 19th century. The location of the gardens is very much part of their appeal, with the steep outcrop of the Great Sugar Loaf Mountain forming a charming backdrop, while the centrepiece is a 90m (272ft) waterfall, claimed to be the highest in Ireland.

ST KEVIN'S BED

Glendalough means 'Glen of the Two Lakes' and a rocky shelf high on the steep south bank of the upper *lough* is said to be St Kevin's bed, where the saint slept to escape an importunate young woman who was in love with him. When she sought him out he shoved her into the lake rather than succumb, thus assuring himself a place in the chronicle of saints.

Below: *Newgrange, one of Europe's most important Stone Age sites.*
Opposite: *The chamber within Newgrange is some 6m (20ft) high.*

COUNTY MEATH

North of County Dublin, County Meath is a region of prosperous, fertile farmland and is one of the cradles of pre-Christian and early Celtic Ireland. The River Boyne flows through the county, meeting the sea at Drogheda.

Slane *

An attractive village of grey stone, terraced houses on streets sloping down to the River Boyne, Slane is close to several of Kildare's historic sights.

Slane Castle *

Built in the 18th century for the Marquess of Conyngham, this imitation-medieval folly with its turrets and battlements is used as a venue for rock concerts. It is privately owned and only the restaurant is open to the public. Open daily, restaurant only.

Hill of Slane *

According to local legend, St Patrick lit a defiant beacon here, within sight of the High King's seat at Tara, to announce the coming of Christianity. He later founded one of Ireland's first churches atop the hill, where the crumbling, unenclosed shell of a 16th-century Franciscan abbey, abandoned in the 17th century, now stands. The only trace of the 6th-century monastery of St Erc, one of Patrick's early converts, is the faint depression around the hill marking the line of its walls.

SAINT PATRICK

Christianity is said to have been brought to Ireland by St Patrick (389–461), who was kidnapped from his Romanized British home as a youth and sold into slavery in Ireland, where he stayed for six years. On his escape and return to Britain, he received a vision ordering him to return to Ireland as a missionary. On the strength of this, he elevated himself to the rank of bishop and on returning to Ireland won the hearts and minds of a number of Irish kings and chiefs. He is also credited with miraculously ridding the island of snakes – of which there are none to this day.

Hill of Tara *

Ireland's answer to Stonehenge, the ceremonial seat of the High Kings of Ireland has been an important site since the Stone Age and was a political and religious centre in early Christian times. With its 2m (6ft) standing stones amid rolling sheep pastures, the hill still has a mystical atmosphere. The magnificent gold **Tara Brooch**, discovered during excavations at the site, is displayed in the National Museum. An interpretative centre is located in the former Church of Ireland church building at the foot of the hill. Open: May–mid-June, daily 10:00–17:00, mid-June–mid-September, daily 09:30–18:30, mid-September–October 10:00–17:00.

Brugh na Boinne (Newgrange, Dowth and Knowth prehistoric tombs) ***

The most fascinating ancient archaeological site in Ireland and one of the most important Stone Age sites in Europe should not be missed. Three tomb clusters, more than 2000 years old, are spread over several square kilometres of land beside the River Boyne.

Newgrange, the most fully excavated and restored tomb site, is as striking as any of the relics of ancient Greece. A tunnel-like passage (not for the claustrophobic) leads into the heart of a great turf-covered stone mound, some 13¹/₂m (40ft) high and 80m (245ft) in diameter. Within is a vast, 6m (20ft) high domed chamber, its walls ringed with mighty boulders carved into the complex curves and spirals typical of Celtic religious art. The neighbouring tomb sites at **Knowth** and **Dowth** are closed to the public, awaiting excavation and restoration. The site is located off the N5 highway 1km (²/₃ miles) east of Slane village. Open year-round.

> ### NEWGRANGE
>
> An eerie event takes place at dawn each winter solstice, 21 December, at Newgrange: the sun shines through a slit in the chamber and eventually moves slowly along the entire passage in order to illuminate it for just 17 minutes. The phenomenon, like so many others, has a rational explanation. The earth's position has moved since the mound was built – originally, the sun light would have lit up the entire chamber at sunrise. As this is a heavily booked up event, an artificial winter sunrise is simulated every day for visitors.

COUNTY KILDARE
Lucan *

This village by the River Liffey used to be a favourite destination for Dubliners escaping the city at weekends, and there are pleasant walks in the Strawberry Beds Valley, along the River Liffey, and along the towpath of the Grand Canal, which passes close by the village.

Above: Surrounded by estate parkland, the K Club course, designed by Arnold Palmer, straddles the scenic River Liffey.

The K Club *

An 18-hole golf course, 50 minutes' drive from Dublin city, off the N4 at Lucan and adjoining the grounds of the 19th-century Straffan House, now the luxurious Kildare Hotel and Country Club. The course is a par 72 and straddles the River Liffey. Opened in 1991, it was designed by Arnold Palmer and is surrounded by ancient estate parkland. Open to visitors weekdays 08:00–13:25 and 14:25 to dusk, weekends 08:00–10:30 and 15:00 to dusk.

CASTLEDERMOT

Castledermot village clusters around a 12th-century castle, now a luxury hotel and country club.

Kilkea Castle Hotel and Golf Club *

The oldest inhabited castle in Ireland, Kilkea was built in 1188 by the Norman knight Hugh de Lacy for his feudal lord, Walter de Riddlesford, only 11 years after the first Anglo-Norman invasion of Ireland. Kilkea Castle passed by marriage to the powerful and contumacious Fitzgerald family. Surrounded by rose gardens, it is now one of Ireland's finest castle-hotels. The 18-hole golf course, a par 71, is one of Ireland's most challenging, with the River Greese to be negotiated on eight holes. Open to guests; golf club open to visitors weekdays, and at weekends by appointment.

MAYNOOTH

Maynooth, on the main N4 highway, is a lively university town on the banks of the Royal Canal.

St Patrick's College and Museum ★★

St Patrick's College was opened as a Catholic seminary in 1795, the first Catholic educational centre to open since the English suppression of the Catholic church in the 16th and 17th centuries. The college's spartan Georgian and early Victorian buildings cluster around two quadrangles, dating from 1795 and 1845. Both are overlooked by the soaring steeple of the college chapel, built in 1875–77. The museum contains a rather peculiar collection of items associated with the college, including the primitive electrical battery invented by the Reverend Dr Nicholas Callan, professor of science at St Patrick's between 1826 and 1864. The oddest exhibit, however, must be the horse-shoeing machine – an invention which would surely have revolutionized transport and agriculture had it not been for the appearance, soon afterwards, of the motor car. Open mid-June–mid-September, Tuesday and Thursday 14:00–16:00, Sunday 14:00–17:00.

> **'THE PARDON OF MAYNOOTH'**
>
> Maynooth Castle, next to St Patrick's College, was the home of the Fitzgerald family until the 17th century. Besieged by the English in the 16th century following a rebellion, its garrison surrendered at the promise of leniency, only to be executed, in an incident which has gone down in history as 'the Pardon of Maynooth'.

Below: *St Patrick's College, Maynooth.*

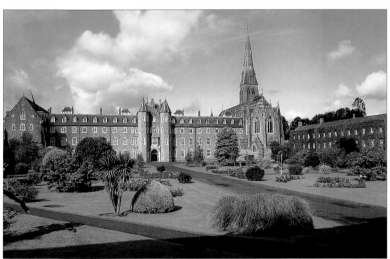

Dublin at a Glance

Street, Dublin 2, tel: 661-8832.
Good value seafood restaurant
close to St Stephen's Green.
Baton Rouge, 119 St
Stephen's Green, Dublin 2, tel:
475-1181. Lively Creole restaurant. Good value lunch/dinner.
Café Caruso, 47 South
William Street, Dublin 2, tel:
677-0708. Offers a choice of
set menus; live piano music.
Bucci Il Ristorante, 7 Lower
Camden Street, Dublin 2, tel:
475-1020. Fine Italian restaurant, excellent value for money
and a good wine list.
Cooke's Café, 14 South
William Street, Dublin 2, tel:
679-0536. Stylish café-restau-
rants with extensive wine list
and interesting Mediterranean/
Californian bill of fare.
Fitzers Restaurant, National
Gallery, Dublin 2, tel: 661-
4496. National Gallery's award-
winning lunchtime restaurant.

BUDGET
Bad Ass Café, 9–11 Crown
Alley, Temple Bar, Dublin 2,
tel: 671-2596. Burger, salad,
pizza and fries restaurant.
Break for the Border,
Johnson's Place, Dublin 2, tel:
478-0300. Burgers and beer in
a cowboy-themed restaurant.
Castle Vaults Bistro, Treasury
Building, Dublin Castle, Dublin
2, tel: 677-0678. Cheap, good
lunches in south Dublin.

North of the Liffey
LUXURY
Aberdeen Restaurant, The
Gresham Hotel, O'Connell

Street, Dublin 1, tel: 874-6881.
Fine restaurant in north
Dublin's best hotel, noted for
its comprehensive wine list.

MID-RANGE
The Bianconi Room, North
Star Hotel, Amiens Street,
Dublin 1, tel: 836-3136. Good
value, fine service, emphasis
on fresh local ingredients.
Chapter One Restaurant,
18–19 Parnell Square, Dublin1,
tel: 873-2266. Unusual menu
blends Irish ingredients with
Scandinavian influences.
Located in basement of
Dublin Writers' Museum.

BUDGET
101 Talbot, 101 Talbot Street,
Dublin 1, tel: 874-5011.
Highly recommended, value
for money Mediterranean
restaurant, good selection of
vegetarian and seafood dishes.

ENTERTAINMENT

Dublin is rich in nightlife,
from traditional music in lively
pubs to the latest in dance,
theatre, and ballet. Take a
walk along Leeson Street,
where Dublin's noisiest
nightlife is to be found.

Traditional music venues
An Beal Bocht, Charlemont
Street, Dublin 2, tel: (01)
475-5614.
The Brazen Head, Bridge
Street, Dublin 8, tel: (01)
677-9549.
The Merchant, Bridge Street,
Dublin 8, tel: (01) 679-3797.

Slattery's, Capel Street,
Dublin1, tel: (01) 872-971.
Mother Redcaps, Back Lane,
Christchurch, Dublin 8, tel:
(01) 453-8306.
O'Donoghue's, Merrion Row,
Dublin 2, tel: (01) 661-4303.
The Mean Fiddler, Wexford
Street, Dublin 2, tel: (01)
475-8555.
The Harcourt Hotel,
Harcourt Street, Dublin 2,
tel: (1850) 664 455.
Kitty O'Shea's, Upper Grand
Canal Street, Dublin 2, tel: (01)
660-9965
The Lower Deck, Portobello,
Dublin 8, tel: (01) 453-4853.

Theatres
Abbey Theatre, Lower Abbey
Street, Dublin 1, tel: (01)
878-7222.
Gaiety Theatre, South King
Street, Dublin 2, tel: (01)
677-1717.
Gate Theatre, Cavendish
Row, Parnell Square, Dublin 1,
tel: (01) 874-4045.

Discos and Nightclubs
Annabel's, Burlington Hotel,
Dublin 4, tel: (01) 660-5222.
Club M, Blooms Hotel,
Anglesea Street, Dublin 2,
tel: (01) 679-0277.
Club Paradiso, Irish Film
Centre, Eustace Street, Dublin
2, tel: (01) 677-8788.
Buck Whalerys, 67 Lower
Leeson Street, Dublin 2,
tel: (01) 676-1755.
Lillies Bordello, Adam Court,
Grafton Street, Dublin 2,
tel: (01) 679-9204.

Dublin at a Glance

Cinemas
Adelphi, Middle Abbey Street, Dublin 1, tel: (01) 873-1161.
Ambassador, Parnell Square, Dublin 1, tel: (01) 872-7000
Irish Film Centre, Eustace Street, Dublin 2, tel: (01) 679-3477.

SHOPPING

Dublin is not a cheap shopping city, as most gift and souvenir purchases are subject to 21% VAT. On the positive side, its shopping streets are not over-whelmed by tatty souvenir shops. Visitors who are not EU residents can claim back VAT in cash on their departure from Ireland using the Cashback vouchers issued by many major Dublin stores.
Among the best buys in Dublin are knitwear, tweeds and fine woollen, mohair and cashmere fabrics; fine Irish linen; Waterford crystal glass-ware; and handcrafted jew-ellery. Look for these on the recently-pedestrianized **Grafton Street**, the city's smartest shopping area, and on **Dawson Street**, running parallel to it, where you will find the city's newest shop-ping mall, **Royal Hibernian Way.** Other up-market shop-ping malls in the city include the **St Stephen's Green Shopping Centre**, at the top of Grafton Street and the **Powerscourt Townhouse Centre** on Clarendon Street, just off Grafton Street. Dublin also has a good selection of

antique dealers, most of which cluster around Francis Street, on the edge of The Liberties in South Dublin.

TOURS AND EXCURSIONS

County Dublin and the neighbouring counties offer fascinating sightseeing and lovely countryside, from the near-wilderness of the Dublin and Wicklow Mountains to the lovely beaches and estuaries of Dublin Bay and the County Dublin coast. A number of companies offer sightseeing tours within Dublin city and to the most popular sightseeing destinations further afield.
Dublin City Tours: Dublin Bus (*Bus Atha Cliath*), 59 Upper O'Connell Street, Dublin 1, tel: (01) 873-4222.
Dublin Bus runs daily tours of the city on open-topped double-decker buses, year round except winter Sundays.
Gogan Travel, 7 South Great George's St, Dublin 2, tel: (01) 679-6444. Offer escorted coach tours of the city with departures on Sunday and sev-eral times weekly year round.
Walking tours: Literary Performance Walking Tour: Visiting the Abbey Theatre, Trinity College, Dublin Castle and Dublin's medieval build-ings, this two-hour tour fea-tures performances by your guide of passages by Yeats, Behan, O'Casey, and other great Dublin writers and characters. Booking: tel/fax: (01) 478-0191.

The Jameson Dublin Literary Pub Crawl: The 2½-hour tour takes you to a selection of Dublin's best-known literary pubs with an entourage of actors who perform from the works of the city's best-known writers. Departs nightly in summer (Easter–October 31) at 19:30; Thursday–Saturday at 19:30 in winter; and year-round on Sundays at 12:00. Starts from The Duke, Duke Street; turn up and join or call (01) 454-0228 for bookings and information.
Limousine Tours: Tours of Dublin by luxury limousine or helicopter with your own guide, tel: (01) 872-3003.
Coach tours:
Gray Line Tours, 3 Clanwilliam Terrace, Grand Canal Quay, Dublin 2, tel: (01) 661-9666. Coach tours to Malahide Castle, Glendalough, Tara and the Boyne Valley as well as Dublin city tours.

USEFUL CONTACTS

Dublin Tourism, offices at 13 Upper O'Connell Street and at Baggot Street Bridge; also at Dun Laoghaire Port Terminal Building and at Dublin International Airport (arrivals hall).
Dublin Tourism Telephone Service, tourist information: tel: (01) 284-4768; fax: 284-1751; local or national credit card reservations, tel: (01) 284-1765.

Travel Tips

Tourist Information

The Irish Tourist Board (*Bord Failte*) maintains overseas offices in London, Belfast, New York, Toronto and Sydney, as well as in Dublin. Bord Failte also has information offices, open year-round, in Dublin at 14 Upper O'Connell Street and at Baggot Street Bridge. Other information desks can be found in the arrivals hall at Dublin International Airport and at the Dun Laoghaire Port Terminal Building.

Embassies and Consulates
In Dublin
Australia: 6th floor, Fitzwilton House, Wilton Terrace, Dublin 2, tel: (01) 676-1517.
Canada: 4th floor, 65-68 St Stephen's Green, Dublin 2, tel: (01) 478-1988.
UK: 31 Merrion Road, Dublin 4, tel: (01) 269-5211.
USA: 42 Elgin Road, Dublin 4, tel: (01) 668-8777.

International
Australia: MLC Centre, 38th Level, Martin Place, Sydney 2000, tel: (02) 232-7177.

Canada: 10 King Street East, Toronto, M5C 1C3, tel: (01) 364-1301.
UK: 150 Bond Street, London W1Y OAQ, tel: (0171) 493-3201.
USA: 757 Fifth Avenue, New York NY 10017, tel: (01) 418-0800.

Entry Requirements

Visas are not required for citizens of European Union countries nor for US, Canadian, Australian, New Zealand or South African nationals intending to stay for less than three months.

Customs

Normal European Union customs requirements apply to visitors arriving in Ireland. Under EU guidelines travellers from other EU countries (except Britain) can bring up to 50 litres of duty-paid beer, 25 litres of wine and 800 cigarettes. Travellers from Britain and from non-EU countries may bring in 200 cigarettes, 1 litre of spirits, 2 litres of wine, 50 grams of perfume and 20cc of toilet water, plus other

dutiable goods to the value of £34 per person, provided all are for personal use only.

Health Requirements

There are no special health requirements for visitors entering Ireland.

Getting There

By Air: There are frequent international flights to Dublin from most major British cities, including all four London airports, Birmingham, Manchester, Liverpool, Glasgow and Edinburgh, by the Irish airlines Aer Lingus and Ryanair and by a number of other carriers. Irish and international airlines also connect the Irish capital with most main European cities and with key gateways in the US and Canada.
By Sea: There are daily ferries to Dublin and to Dun Laoghaire, Dublin's alternative ferry terminus, from Holyhead in Wales.
By Road: The main north road N1 connects Dublin with Northern Ireland and its capital, Belfast.

By Rail: There are several trains daily each way between Dublin and Belfast in Northern Ireland, and frequent rail services to other regional cities in the Republic of Ireland.

What to Pack
Everyday wear will depend on when you go, but given Dublin's unpredictable climate you should always pack a waterproof coat or jacket and comfortable wet-weather footwear. A hat or umbrella will be welcome in summer and essential in winter. Be prepared for colder weather from September to May. A sweater will be useful at any time of the year. Dress codes in restaurants, nightspots and hotels are relaxed, and smart casual wear is acceptable for virtually any occasion; business travellers, however, will probably wish to pack the usual business attire.

Money Matters
Currency: The Irish punt (pound) is worth a fraction less than 1.00 sterling/US $1.50. The punt is divided into 100 pennies, with coins in 1p, 2p, 5p, 10p, 20p and 50p denominations and notes in £1, £5, £10, £20, £50, and £100.
Changing money: Banks are open 10:00–12:30 and 13:30–15:00, Monday to Friday. Larger hotels will also change money or traveller's cheques in major currencies for guests.

Bank of Ireland, 34 College Green, Dublin 2, tel: (01) 679-3777.
Allied Irish Bank, O'Connell Street, Dublin1, tel: (01) 873-0555.
American Express Travel Service, 116 Grafton Street, Dublin 2, tel: (01) 677-2874.
American Express Travel Service, 14 Upper O'Connell Street, Dublin 1, tel: (01) 878-6892.
JWT ForEx, 69 Upper O'Connell Street, Dublin 1, tel: (01) 67 2874.
Traveller's cheques: American Express Travel Service, 116 Grafton Street, Dublin 2, tel: (01) 677-2874; lost or stolen cheques, tel: (01 800) 626-000.
Credit Cards: All major credit cards and charge cards are accepted in larger stores, hotels and restaurants, but smaller establishments prefer payment in cash. American Express (see Traveller's Cheques, above); Access, Mastercard and Visa are handled by Bank of Ireland, Nassau Street, Dublin 1; lost or stolen cards, tel: (01 850) 706 706.
Tipping: A 10% tip will be welcomed by taxi drivers, hotel porters and table staff in restaurants and cafés, but tipping is not usual in bars.
Tax: Visitors from outside the European Union may reclaim Value Added Tax (VAT) on purchases (though not on services) under the Cashback scheme which operates in larger, tourist-oriented shops, especially

those catering to North American visitors. These shops display a conspicuous 'Cashback' logo and issue vouchers which are exchanged for cash refunds at the Cashback desk in Dublin International Airport departure hall.

Accommodation
Dublin has a wide range of accommodation to suit all needs and budgets, though large international chain hotels are outnumbered by individual, locally-owned and locally-managed hotels. The Irish Tourist Board, in co-operation with the Irish Hotel Federation, operates a two-tier hotel classification system for hotels and guesthouses, rating them from one to five stars.
Guesthouses are not required to offer as wide a range of services and facilities as hotels, but this does not mean that guesthouse accommodation is necessarily inferior. Quality controls are strict, and many guesthouses offer standards well in excess of the requirements for each category. Guesthouse accommodation can be very good value for money, and many visitors find the more personal welcome in these properties – many of which are family-run – to be warmer than in bigger hotels.

Eating Out
Eating out in Dublin can be an expensive proposition as most restaurants are subject

to the highest rate of Value Added Tax (VAT) at 21%. Dublin's peculiar liquor licensing laws complicate the picture still further, and wine drinkers will find the price of even an undistinguished bottle staggeringly high. Restaurants range from upmarket old establishments which hark back to Dublin's elegant heyday to noisy, jumping nightspots favoured by Dublin's younger set. Most ethnic cuisines are well represented, and Dublin in the 1990s has taken European-style café society to its heart, with a sprinkling of popular café-bars catering to the hip and the trendy. For good-value, budget-eating places of all kinds, try the newly-fashionable **Temple Bar** area or the places around **Trinity College**, where restaurants and bars cater to penny-conscious students. For elegant (and expensive) wining and dining, try the fine restaurants in Dublin's first-class hotels, or head for the upmarket suburb of **Ballsbridge**, where many of the city's most cosmopolitan establishments are clustered.

Transport

Air: Within Ireland, distances are so short that there is little point in air travel, though there are air connections between Dublin and Ireland's second city, Cork.

Rail and Bus: Main-line trains go from two central stations: Connolly, for

---

USEFUL PHRASES

Dubliners speak their own kind of English, loaded with a vocabulary of slang unique to the city. Visitors attempting to communicate in Irish will find themselves greeted at best with incomprehension and at worst with the kind of cutting sarcasm which is another Dublin speciality. However, there is one word of Irish which is absolutely essential – **slainte**, pronounced 'slansha'. It means 'cheers' and in the home of Guinness you should use it frequently.

---

services to the north, northwest and east, and Heuston for all services to the west, south, southwest and southeast.
Connolly Station, Amiens St, Dublin 1, tel: (01) 836-3333.
Heuston Station, Kingsbridge, Dublin 8, tel: (01) 836-3333.
General inquiries, tel: (01) 836-6222.
Bus: Bus Eireann (Irish Bus) operates bus services from

Dublin to all points around Ireland. Buses depart from Eblana Busaras (Dublin Bus Station), Store Street, at the corner of Beresford Place and Amiens Street, 200m (650ft) south of Connolly Railway Station.
Bus Eireann, 59 Upper O'Connell Street, Dublin 1, tel: (01) 836-6111.
Car: Car rental is pointless if you plan to stay within Dublin city. However, for those planning to explore County Dublin and its neighbouring counties or to travel further afield, car rental is available both in the city centre and at Dublin International Airport. For those travelling with their own vehicles, many hotels and guesthouses offer free off-street parking. Driving licenses issued elsewhere in the European Union are valid. Non-EU visitors need an International Driving Licence, obtainable on arrival through motoring organizations or before you leave home. When renting a car, full collision damage waiver (CDW) and liability

---

CONVERSION CHART		
FROM	**TO**	**MULTIPLY BY**
Millimetres	Inches	0.0394
Metres	Yards	1.0936
Metres	Feet	3.281
Kilometres	Miles	0.6214
Kilometres square	Square miles	0.386
Hectares	Acres	2.471
Litres	Pints	1.760
Kilograms	Pounds	2.205
Tonnes	Tons	0.984
To convert Celsius to Fahrenheit: x 9 ÷ 5 + 32		

insurance is recommended. Drive on the right and observe speed limits of 50kph (30mph) in towns and 118kph (70mph) on highways. Rear seat and front seat passengers and drivers must wear seatbelts. Bringing your own vehicle by sea from the UK or Europe is simple. You need registration documents, proof of insurance valid for the Republic of Ireland (European Green card), driving licence or international permit. However, your car may not be driven by an Irish resident during your visit, other than by a garage employee with your written permission. Tour operators arranging motoring holidays with accommodation throughout Ireland include The Irish Selection, Chester Close, London SW1X 7BQ, tel: (0171) 245-0055, fax: 259-6093.

Business Hours
Banks are open 10:00–12:30 and 13:30–15:00, Monday to Friday. Most shops are open 09:00–17:30, with late opening until 20:00 on Thursdays.

Time
Ireland uses Greenwich Meridien Time (GMT) in winter and GMT + 1 hour in summer.

Communications
The area dialling code of Dublin is (01) for calls within the Republic of Ireland and (00 353 1) for calls from

---

PUBLIC HOLIDAYS AND FESTIVALS

1 January ●
New Year's Day
17 March ●
St Patrick's Day
Good Friday
Easter Monday
25 December ●
Christmas Day
26 December ●
St Stephen's Day
as well as three holidays in June, August and October which vary from year to year.
Visitors from the USA, where St Patrick's Day is a major event in many places, may be surprised to find that is not regarded as a big day of celebration in Dublin.

---

abroad. To call the operator tel: 114; directory enquiries tel: 1198; international calls may be made from any public phone through the operator.

Electricity
Electrical supply is 220V. Most hotels have dual 220/110V sockets for hair dryers and razors.

Weights and Measures
Like the UK, Ireland – despite having been a member of the European Community/ European Union for more than 20 years – is still in the throes of conversion to the metric system. Although measurements are officially metric,

---

many people still think in terms of miles rather than kilometres and pounds and ounces rather than kilograms and grams, and any drinker asking for 500 millilitres of Guinness instead of a pint will get some very odd looks!

Health Precautions
No special health precautions are required when travelling in Ireland.

Health Services
European Union residents holding an E111 certificate, available from your doctor or health department before departure, are entitled to free treatment.
24-hour Doctor on Duty service, tel: (01) 453-9333.

Safety and Security
Dublin has a relatively high crime rate as a result of widespread youth unemployment and one of the worst hard drug addiction rates in Europe. Violent crime against visitors, however, is relatively rare, as is theft from hotel rooms. However, theft from vehicles, pick-pocketing and handbag snatching are not uncommon and caution should be observed.

Emergencies
Police, fire, ambulance, and lifeboat service, tel: **999**.

Etiquette
No special requirements or unusual local conventions.

Language

Despite more than a century of strenuous efforts to revive Irish as the national language, English – albeit with a strong Irish tinge – is the first language of Ireland and Dublin. Attempts to communicate in Irish are more than likely to be met with baffled incomprehension or outright laughter.

Travel with Gulliver

The Irish Tourist Board operates a computerised reservation and information system called Gulliver. Available at all main tourist information offices, it gives up-to-the-minute information on events and attractions in Dublin and throughout Ireland, as well as booking accommodation in hotels, guesthouses, town and country homes, farmhouses, and university halls of residence. It also organises tours, river and canal cruises and car rental.

Road signs

Road signs in Dublin and throughout Ireland are the standard set of symbols, numerals and signage in use throughout the European Union and are immediately easy to decipher even if you are not yet familiar with them. Street signs are in English.

Best buys

Dublin is not a cheap city, as European cities go, but high-quality souvenirs on offer in a variety of speciality shops include Georgian, Victorian and Edwardian antiques; silver,

watches and jewellery old and new; antiquarian books from one of the city's many booksellers; woollen knitwear and Irish linen; pewter, crystal glassware and fine porcelain. Irish whiskey, in a variety of ages and blends, is another good buy.

Musical Pub Crawl

Learn about Irish music in its native environment on the Dublin Musical Pub Crawl, led by two professional musicians who perform while telling the story of Irish music and its influences on contemporary music around the world. The tour starts in **Oliver St John Gogarty's** in Temple Bar at 19:30 every night except Saturday and lasts approximately 2½ hours,

taking in a selection of Dublin's best pubs and finishing with a session of traditional music. For bookings and information, tel/fax: 478 0191.

Heritage Passport

If you plan intensive sightseeing, invest in the very helpful '*Dublin Alive Alive O*', a concession guide to Dublin's main sights, which offers a 10% reduction on entry costs to Dublinia, the Dublin Writers Museum, Dublin Zoo, the Guinness Hop Store, the Irish Museum of Modern Art, Malahide Castle, the National Museum of Ireland, Newman House, Temple Bar attractions and Trinity College. It costs £2 and is available from tourist information offices and participating attractions.

GOOD READING

Roddy Doyle, *The Snapper* (1990), *The Commitments* (1988), *The Van* (1991), also published as *The Barrytown Trilogy* (1992) and *Paddy Clark Ha Ha Ha* (1993), all in Minerva.
James Joyce, *Dubliners* (1914); *Portrait of the Artist as a young Man* (1916); *Ulysses* (1922), all in Penguin.
Peter Neville, *A Traveller's History of Ireland* (1993).
Flann O'Brien, *The Third Policeman, The Dalkey Archive, At-Swin-Two-Birds* and *The Hard Life*, all in Picador; and as **Myles na gCopaleen**, *The Best of Myles*, also in Picador.
Gemma Hussey, *Ireland Today* (1993), Viking.

Fergus Finlay, Mary Robinson, A president with a Purpose (1990), O'Brien Press.
Robert Kee, *Ireland, A History* (1982, reprinted and revised 1995), Abacus.
Nathanieal Harris, *The Easter Rising* (1987), Dryad Press.
Richard Kearney, *Across the Frontiers: Ireland in the 1990s* (1988), Wolfhouse Press.
Gabriel Fitzmaurice (ed), *Irish Poetry Now* (1993), Wolfhound Press.
Peter Fallon and Derek Mahon (ed), *Penguin Book of Contemporary Irish Poetry* (1990), Penguin.
Frank McDonald, *The Destruction of Dublin* (1985), Gill & McMillan.

INDEX